BUSINESS OPPORTUNITIES IN SICHUAN PROVINCE, CHINA

IT IS INDEED not an easy task understanding the very complicated business structures and cultures of the vastly different states in China. The coordinated efforts of the authors in putting together what all businessmen would need to know when investing in China must be recommended. They have done a formidable job of interpreting business opportunities in a Chinese environment. The main ingredients for business such as the capital structure, investment regulations, tax structure, financial structure and business forms are aptly addressed in this book. In short, the book has put together in a concise form the basic information that one needs, to take the first step in exploring business opportunities in Sichuan Province, an up-and-coming part of China.

JASON LIM KOK ENG (VICE-GENERAL MANAGER, AUROCOMP GROUP, SINGAPORE)

Titles in the Nanyang Business Report Series

Business Opportunities in Penang, Malaysia

Business Opportunities in Sichuan Province, China

Business Opportunities in India

Business Opportunities in the Philippines

Business Opportunities in Myanmar

Business Opportunities in the Yangtze River Delta, China

For further enquiries, information or feedback on the series, please write to the Editor at e-mail: prenhall@singnet.com.sg or Simon & Schuster (Asia) Pte Ltd, 317 Alexandra Road, #04-01 IKEA Building, Singapore 159965.

NANYANG BUSINESS REPORT SERIES

Business Opportunities in Sichuan Province China

Edited by

Tan Teck Meng (Dean)
Low Aik Meng (Vice Dean and Director of MBA Programme)
Chew Soon Beng (Head, Applied Economics)
John J. Williams (Chief Coordinator, Business Study Mission)
Cao Yong (Coordinator, Business Study Mission)
Chen Kang (Coordinator, Business Study Mission)

Nanyang Technological University
Singapore

Prentice Hall
Singapore New York London Toronto Sydney Tokyo

First published 1996 by
Prentice Hall
Simon & Schuster (Asia) Pte Ltd
317 Alexandra Road
#04-01 IKEA Building
Singapore 159965

Printed in Singapore

1 2 3 4 5 00 99 98 97 96

ISBN 0-13-713223-9
ISBN 0-13-267881-0 (pbk)

Prentice Hall International (UK) Limited, *London*
Prentice Hall of Australia Pty. Limited, *Sydney*
Prentice Hall Canada Inc., *Toronto*
Prentice Hall Hispanoamericana, *S.A., Mexico*
Prentice Hall of India Private Limited, *New Delhi*
Prentice Hall of Japan, Inc., *Tokyo*
Editora Prentice Hall do Brasil, Ltda., *Rio de Janeiro*
Prentice Hall, Inc., *Upper Saddle River, New Jersey*

CONTENTS

ABOUT THE EDITORS

TAN TECK MENG is Professor and Dean at the Nanyang Business School. Since joining academia in the early 1970s, Professor Tan has combined his university responsibilities with extensive consultancy work, largely in the field of accountancy. He holds senior positions on a number of institutional boards and committees in Singapore including the Accounting and Auditing Services Working Group of the Economic Committee, the Public Accountants Board, the Board of Directors of Singapore Reinsurance Corporation Limited, the Institute of Certified Public Accountants of Singapore (ICPAS) Annual Report Award Competition Committee and the Income Tax Board of Review. Professor Tan is founding Director of the Entrepreneurship Development Centre (ENDEC) and in 1992 was elected to the Board of Governors of the MIT Sloan School of Management Society for Senior Executives. He is a council member of the ICPAS.

LOW AIK MENG is Associate Professor and Director of the MBA programme at the Nanyang Business School. He worked for five years as an accountant and an internal auditor before joining academia in 1975. He was Vice-Dean of the Faculty of Accountancy and Business Administration at the National University of Singapore until he joined the Nanyang Technological University in 1987. He is currently Vice-Dean at the Nanyang Business School and has been the Director of its very successful MBA Programme since its inception in 1991. Under his leadership, the MBA Programme has been building a network of contacts with businesses and government bodies in Singapore and overseas. He spearheads the thrice-yearly Business Study Missions which are an integral part of the MBA

Programme. Associate Professor Low continues to be active in the accountancy profession and serves on several committees in the Institute of Certified Public Accountants of Singapore.

CHEW SOON BENG is Associate Professor and Head of the Applied Economics Division at the Nanyang Business School. He is also the Director of the Asian Commerce and Economics Studies Centre (ACES) which conducts Mandarin executive programmes for senior officials from China and tourism management programmes for senior officials from Vietnam. Dr. Chew has been a consultant to the Internal Labour Organisation and the Asian Development Bank. He is author of, *inter alia*, *Small Firms in Singapore* (Oxford University Press, 1988), *Trade Unionism in Singapore* (McGraw Hill, 1990), and *The Employment-Driven Industrial Relations Regimes* (Avebury, 1995).

JOHN J. WILLIAMS is Associate Professor at the Nanyang Business School and Chief Coordinator of the MBA Business Study Mission programme. He has taught and carried out research projects in several countries including Canada, the U.S., Kenya and Singapore. Throughout the latter part of the 1980s, Dr. Williams served as Vice-Chairman and Chairman of the Final Accreditation Exam Board for the Society of Management Accountants of Canada, which admitted him as a Fellow in the Society in 1992. Although active in consulting for government agencies in the U.S. and Canada during this period, he has published extensively in leading academic and professional journals and he continues to pursue the study of emerging regional economies in the Asean region.

CAO YONG is Lecturer at the Nanyang Business School and Head, Chinese Economic Study Unit, ACES. Dr. Cao Yong received his PhD degree from the Australian National University. He was a research economist for the Institute of Economics of the Chinese Academy of Social Sciences and the Australian National University. He started his study on the Chinese economy in 1982 when he joined the Chinese Academy of Social Sciences in Beijing. Since then, he has participated in many study missions in China and has had intensive contacts with Chinese enterprises and economic organisations. His research interest is on the reforms of Chinese industrial enterprise and Chinese business practice. He has published papers in the *Journal of Applied Economics, Asian Economic Journal, Economic Systems, Journal of Far Eastern Business, Accounting and Business Review, Jingji Yangjiu* (Economic Research) and other international journals and books.

CHEN KANG is a Lecturer at the Nanyang Business School. Before joining Nanyang Technological University, Dr. Chen worked for the World Bank's Socialist Economies Reform Unit as an economist and subsequently taught at the National University of Singapore. He has published in a number of international journals in the areas of macroeconometric modelling, the economic reform of China, and other transitional economies. He is the author of the *Chinese Economy in Transition: Micro Changes and Macro Implications* (Singapore University Press, 1995).

PREFACE

The Master of Business Administration (MBA) programme of the Nanyang Business School at Nanyang Technological University requires participants to complete a Business Study Mission (BSM) before graduation. The purpose of these visits to other countries is to expose MBA participants to business opportunities and the realities of doing business in cultural environments different from Singapore.

The information presented in this book is a culmination of the business reports arising from the MBA Business Study Mission to Sichuan Province, China during the period 11–21 June 1994. Without doubt, the Chinese economy is expanding in unprecedented ways by any world standards. While considerably more investment knowledge currently exists on the economic expansion taking place in China's coastal cities, relatively less is known about investment opportunities in inner China. Thus, the inner cities of Chengdu, Chongqing and Wuhan are potential markets for Singapore firms contemplating doing business in China.

Not unexpectedly, one of the barriers to understanding the investment potential in Sichuan Province was the dearth of English language material, in any form of publication, inside or outside the boundaries of China. Thus, much of the material presented in this volume was distilled through translated documents in Mandarin or through translated seminars, discussions and personal interviews with government officials, local academics and important leaders of the Sichuan business community. To our knowledge, these sources have contributed a rich set of information which is unavailable elsewhere.

Editors:
TAN Teck Meng
LOW Aik Meng
CHEW Soon Beng
John J. WILLIAMS
CAO Yong
CHEN Kang

ACKNOWLEDGEMENTS

Bringing a 40-member delegation to Sichuan province, China, required the commitment and dedication of many Chinese officials and business people. First, we thank the Executive Vice Mayor of Chengdu, Mr. Xiao Zu Xiu, for his warm hospitality and supporting our visit to the Jingliuba Economic and Technological Development Zone. Thanks also to Professor Yang Gang, Executive Director of the Institute of Economic Reform in the Sichuan Academy of Social Sciences, for hosting the seminars on foreign investment policy and reforms of the financial system in China and Professor Zeng Kang Ling, Director of Finance, Society of China, for delivering an excellent seminar paper on these issues.

We wish to express our appreciation to Mr. Shang Ai, General Secretary of the Chongqing Municipal Government for welcoming us to the city of Chongqing and hosting a series of seminars on its economy and various joint venture experiences in Chongqing, and supporting our visit to the Nanping Economic and Technological Development Zone, including various industrial enterprises. Thanks are extended to all of the many speakers and business people who attended and participated in the seminars.

We are most grateful to Mr. Xie Chen Mong and Mr. Ma Chang Ming, Senior Administrative Officials from the Chongqing Municipal Government, for their time and informative discussions while accompanying the Business Study Mission down the Yangtze River from Chongqing to Wuhan. Also, thanks to all the people at the Guozhouba hydroelectric power dam and from the commercial and industrial areas of Wuhan for enlightening our understanding of investment opportunities in the region.

Finally, thanks to all of our MBA participants for their diligent efforts in gathering information from translated Mandarin documents, to the MBA Office, to Grace Cheng and Adelene Ang for keeping the trip running smoothly, and to Alison Soo for her efforts in bringing this book to completion.

GENERAL ENVIRONMENT

Chapter 1

Investment Climate and Opportunities in South-east China

BY
TAN Teck Meng
LOW Aik Meng
CHEW Soon Beng
John J. WILLIAMS
CAO Yong
CHEN Kang

IN THIS VOLUME, various issues related to foreign direct investment in China are studied from the point of view of potential investors with particular references to Chengdu and Chongqing in Sichuan province. The issues studied can be classified into the following five categories: (1) China's investment environment in general, and the taxation and financial systems in particular; (2) choice of viable investment locations; (3) choice of appropriate industrial sectors for investment; (4) choice of suitable forms of investment; and (5) in depth case studies.

Chapter 2 examines the Chinese taxation system, with particular emphasis on the tax reforms implemented in 1994. It focuses on corporation tax, value added tax, and tax incentives in China's special investment areas. It also compares China's tax system with that of other countries. Furthermore, the authors examine how foreign firms can reduce the tax impact and minimise tax burdens by choosing the appropriate capital structure which allows firms to benefit most from the tax incentives offered.

Two papers deal with China's financial and banking systems. Chapter 3 provides an overview of the banking and financial systems in China. It also studies the various types of bank loans available to foreign investors, with particular focus on loans extended by the Bank of China. It is found that bank loans, in general, are not easily accessible to foreign investors, and the availability of funds is very sensitive to changes in the government's macroeconomic policy. Therefore, foreign investors should not rely heavily on funds raised inside China to finance their investment projects or business operations.

However, there are important factors that can significantly affect the success of foreign investors in obtaining bank loans in China. Chapter 4 studies the vital factors for obtaining bank loans in China. These include some location-specific and industry-specific advantages as well as the advantages of using available collateral, such as land use rights, to secure bank loans. The authors also argue that when formulating strategies of investment financing, decision makers should take into consideration relevant factors such as banking sector reforms, foreign exchange controls, interest differentials, and sources of foreign currency for repayment.

One important lesson learnt by the participants of the MBA Business Mission is that while it is important to understand the general investment environment in China, it is equally important to understand the regional and sectoral differences because of the huge geographic and economic size of China. Chapter 5 studies the investment environment in the inland regions, and seeks to compare it with that of the coastal regions. It points out that China's vast inland area can be an attractive site for foreign investment due to its rich natural resources, abundant supply of labour and land, and huge domestic markets. Of course, inland regions suffer from the problems of higher transportation costs, relatively backward infrastructure and less developed financial markets. However, governments of inland regions have invested an enormous amount of resources into the development of local transportation and infrastructure in recent years. It is argued that for investment projects in industries such as natural resource extractions, infrastructure development related industries, and consumer goods production, advantages in the inland regions can outweigh the disadvantages, especially when land and labour become more expensive in the coastal regions.

Chapter 6 deals with another paper on the issue of investment location. It compares the investment opportunities between two most developed cities of the Sichuan province, i.e., Chengdu and Chongqing, by using the SWOT (strengths, weaknesses, opportunities, threats) paradigm. While it is possible to identify some differences in location-specific factors, the authors acknowledge that such differences may not be important because a new highway between Chengdu and Chongqing was completed at the end of 1995. The new expressway cuts the distance between the two cities from 505 kilometres to 300 kilometres and reduces the travel time between the two cities from 12 hours to a mere 3 hours. Soon the two cities will be interconnected by highways, railways and airways. These changes will make factors of production, such as labour and raw materials, highly mobile and render the problem of choosing one of the two cities for investment a trivial one.

In an effort to study the industry-specific factors with regard to foreign direct investment, Chapter 7 focuses its analysis on three industrial sectors: property development, manufacturing and services. The study of the first two sectors is carried out in the context of Chengdu and Chongqing while the coverage of the third sector is more general in terms of its geographic relevance. The authors recognise that while the rates of return for property development projects are high, risks associated with market uncertainties and policy changes are also high. Car manufacturing and machinery are two manufacturing industries identified by the authors to be the sectors with good investment prospects because they fit well into the cities environment in terms of large numbers of supporting industries, low labour costs, and large untapped domestic markets. In terms of service sectors, the study looks into three particular sectors, namely the advertising industry, management consultancy services and financial services.

Chapter 8 studies the investment prospect of the electronics industry. The relocation of labour-intensive electronics manufacturing plants to China is already an ongoing process because many producers have sought to benefit from China's low cost labour. However, by dividing the industry into three subsectors – consumer electronics, component electronics, and industrial electronics – the author is able to analyse in more detail the market demand and other relevant information on making investment decisions in this particular industry. The author argues that the relocation of production lines to China will actually benefit Singapore's electronic industry although low-grade low-value added local electronic companies will be "blown away in the first storm".

Choosing the right form of investment is at least as important as

form of business investment? By studying each option using information, knowledge, and impression gained from the mission, including a field visit to a factory in Chongqing which produces similar products, the author is able to provide some concrete recommendations to the MNC.

Because of time constraint and the huge size of China, conclusions drawn from this mission can only be viewed as tentative and primitive. However, there is one thing that all mission participants would never fail to agree on and that is, in China's inland areas, there are tremendous investment opportunities awaiting entrepreneurs from home and abroad.

Chapter 2

The Chinese Taxation System and Regulations and their Impact on Foreign Investors' Capital Structure

BY
SOH Szu Wei
CHAN Yin Wan

INTRODUCTION

WITH THE OPENING and transformation of the Chinese economy into a more market oriented economy, the Chinese Government is gradually implementing a comprehensive taxation system. Compared to other developed market economies, the taxation system in China is relatively primitive. This is because the concept of income tax legislation is new in China as foreign entities only began to venture into China after 1978. In addition, the surge of foreign investment[1] into China is a recent occurrence. As such, there is an ambiguity of statutes and lack of precedence in the Chinese taxation system.

China levies individual taxes. This is imposed on foreign individuals and Chinese nationals whose income are derived from Chinese sources. Individuals in this category are subject to the PRC Individual Income Tax law

[1] FDI in 1993 was reported to be in excess of US$100 billion, Source: *The China Daily*.

which was streamlined and came into effect on 1 January 1994.

Apart from individual taxes, other direct and indirect taxes are also imposed. These include the Unified Income Tax (UIT), Customs Duties, Value Added Tax (VAT), Real Estate Tax (RET), Product Tax, Stamp Tax, Capital Gains Tax, Land Use Tax and the Vehicle and Vessel Licence Tax.

Currently, taxation contributes about 80% of China's state revenues compared to 46% in 1978.[2] As China moves towards a market economy, she is motivated by the need to increase public revenue, to use taxation as a mechanism for realising the country's goals and to bring her taxation system in line with international standards. These factors have been attributed to the recent introduction of laws which affect all tax entities including foreigners.

As there has been a significant amount of change in the Chinese taxation system in recent years, much of the past literature is now obsolete. As such, the findings from this paper are derived mainly from the attempt to gather more current information from periodicals and new databases. The new tax system is still being interpreted and, as such, the final impact and effect on companies is still an open question.

This chapter examines the various forms of foreign investment enterprises, the Chinese taxation system, and their impact on foreign investors' capital structure.

FOREIGN INVESTMENT ENTERPRISES (FIE)

FIEs in China may take a number of forms including equity and co-operative joint ventures and wholly owned foreign-owned enterprises. The differences are highlighted in Table 2-1.

Other business and investment forms are representative offices, leasing and licensing arrangements, compensation trade arrangements, counter trade arrangements, processing and assembly agreements, direct sales organisations and enterprises issuing B and H shares.

---

2 It should be noted that the dramatic increase in percentage terms was mainly due to the reform that converted the profits submitted by the state-owned enterprises to the state into tax.

Territoriality

PRC adopts the territoriality concept in its tax collection. As such, corporate income tax is levied on a foreign investment enterprise (FIE) on a consolidated basis regardless of the location where the income is earned. However, foreign tax credits are allowed for income taxes paid to other inland revenue authorities of other countries. This is only granted to the income which is subject to relevant income tax imposed outside China. Foreign enterprises (FEs) are also subject to income tax for income derived from sources in China. However, the derivation of tax is dependent on the status of the FEs. For FEs with establishments in China, they are subject to corporate tax on all income. However, for FEs with no establishments in China, a withholding tax of 20% is imposed.

TABLE 2-1
The Forms of Foreign Investment Enterprises in China

	Equity Joint Ventures	**Co-operative Joint Ventures**	**Wholly Foreign-owned Enterprises**[3]
Tax Code	Law on Joint Venture Using Chinese & Foreign Investment	Chinese-Foreign Co-operation Joint Venture Law	Tax Law of the People's Republic of China on Enterprises with Foreign Investment and Foreign Enterprises
Foreign Equity	Minimum of 25%	Flexible	100%
Equity Investment Forms	Cash, equipment, technology & industrial property rights and other assets	Buildings, equipment, land use rights, intellectual property, etc.	Not applicable
Profit Distribution	According to equity participation	Flexible	Not applicable
Minimum Investment	RMB 1 million	Not applicable	Not applicable

---

3 Restricted to companies operating within the Special Economic Zones and Economic & Technology Development Zones.

CORPORATE INCOME TAX

The term "establishments" is broadly defined in China to cover place of management, branch, office, factory, workshop, mine, oil and gas well, place of extraction of natural resources, building site or construction, assembly, installation or exploration project, place of provision of labour services and business agents. The term "business agents" refer to:

(i) agents who are authorised to conclude purchase contracts on behalf of the principal and who habitually exercise such authority;
(ii) agents who have concluded an agency agreement or contract with the principal and have a stock of goods belonging to the principal on hand with which regular deliveries are made; or
(iii) agents who have the authority to conclude or accept sales contracts on behalf of the principal and who habitually exercise such authority.

Unified Income Tax (UIT)

In China, all forms of FIEs and joint ventures are subjected to the UIT. The UIT replaces the Joint Venture Income Tax (JVIT) and the Foreign Enterprise Income Tax (FEIT) as from 1 July 1991. FIEs and FEs are taxed at the different corporate rates of 15%, 24% and 33% (30% plus a 3% local tax). The tax rates applicable are dependent on the location of the investment.

Companies which operate in the Special Economic Zones[4] (SEZs), Economic & Technology Development Zones[5] (ETDZs), Pudong New Development Zone (PNDZ), Sino-foreign joint venture in port development, foreign & Sino-foreign joint ventures in the financial sector[6], investments in advanced technology projects in designated industrial parks, infrastructure projects in PNDZ and the open cities are charged 15%. Other projects are approved by the State Council.

FIEs located in the Coastal Open Economic Zones[7] (COEZs) and

---

[4] Shenzhen, Zhuhai, Shantou, Xiamen, Hainan.

[5] Behai, Dalian, Fuzhou, Guangzhou, Lianyungang, Nantong, Ningbo, Qingdao, Qinhuangdao, Shanghai, Tianjin, Wenzhou, Yanati, Zhanjiang.

[6] Investment amount must exceed US$10 million and be located in the SEZs, ETDZs and PNDZ.

[7] Liaodong Peninsula, Shandong Peninsula, Changjiang, Pearl River Delta, Southern Fujian.

the 14 open cities are subject to a tax rate of 24%. In addition, a 3% local income tax is imposed by the local tax authorities. However, this can be waived upon application by the FIEs. All other FIEs and FEs with establishments in China other than those above are subject to a tax rate of 33% (30% plus a 3% local tax).

Definition of Income

"Business income" is defined as income from production and business operations. Business operations include industry, mining, transportation, construction, agriculture, forestry, animal husbandry, aquatic industries, commerce, banking and financial services, service and others. "Other incomes" are defined as dividends, interest, income derived from lease or sale of property, royalties, transfer of proprietary technology, patents, technical know-how, trademarks and copyrights and other non-business income.

In China, capital gains are treated as ordinary income. They are therefore subject to corporate income tax. For large projects, the tax entity may opt for "percentage of completion" or "completed contract" methods in reporting earned income. A tax rate of 5% of gross income is assessed for FEs engaged in international transportation and shipping. In addition, FEs are also subject to the UIT.

THE CHINESE TAXATION SYSTEM AND REGULATIONS

Value Added Tax (VAT)

With the tax reforms introduced in 1994, the Consolidated Industrial and Commercial Tax (CICT) has been replaced by the VAT. Foreigners in China will have to pay the VAT which is levied at 13% on food, water, and fuel. For other products, the rate is 17%. Export goods are exempted from the VAT.

Real Estate Tax (RET)

With the recent interest in the real estate market in China, the RET was introduced. The RET is levied on land and building owners in the urban areas. It is based on the rent received or the value of the property.

Stamp Tax

China imposes a stamp tax of between 0.005 to 0.1% of the taxable value of a transaction for legal documents obtained and/or executed by PRC nationals or foreigners.

Capital Gains Tax

A capital gains tax was introduced in the latter part of 1994. The impact will likely be the greatest on property transactions. Currently, the proposed rates range from 30 to 60% on a progressive application. The aim is to control inflation brought on by the property boom.

Provision of Losses

Allowances for doubtful debts are allowed for financial institutions. However, this is subject to the approval of the local tax authorities and it is not to exceed 30% of the outstanding accounts. This is not extended to companies in other sectors. Exchange rate gains or losses are reflected in the profit and loss statements.

Operating losses may be carried forward for a period not exceeding five years. No carry-back provision is allowed. Foreign companies who incur losses from abandoned projects may use these to offset future profits from other sources of income.

Foreign Tax Credit

FIEs which pay tax on income derived from overseas sources may claim tax credits. However, the credit is subject to China's corporate income tax rate. Excess credits may be carried forward for a period of ten years. Foreign tax paid for dividends, rental income and royalties are treated as deductible and not as a tax credit.

Double Taxation Agreements

To date, China has signed 30[8] Double Taxation Agreements. The agreement with Singapore allows for the following withholding tax rates:

---

8 Countries from the CIS are counted as one country.

(a) Dividends[9] 12%
(b) Interest[10] 10%
(c) Royalties 10%

Tax Incentives

Although China has a large market, she still has to compete with other countries to attract foreign direct investment. As such, several tax incentives and tax holidays are offered to investors, subject to approval. These are:

(i) **Five-year Tax Holiday:** This applies to FIEs intending to operate for more than ten years in the manufacturing sector. Tax exemption is granted for the first two years of profit. This is followed by a 50% reduction in tax for the subsequent three years.
(ii) **Additional Ten-year Reduction:** A reduction of 15–30% of the tax rate may be granted upon the expiration of the above.
(iii) **Export-oriented and Technologically Advanced Enterprises:** FIEs which export more than 70% of total production and enterprises which introduce advanced technology into China are allowed to apply for a 50% tax reduction upon expiration of the initial five-year tax holiday. For technologically advanced enterprises, this incentive is available for an additional three years.
(iv) **Other Preferred Investment Projects:** Infrastructure development projects in Hainan SEZ and the PNDZ and Sino-foreign joint ventures in port development are entitled to a five-year 50% tax reduction from the first profit year. However, the project must have an operating period of 15 years. Service FIEs with a total investment value of more than US$5 million and an operational period of ten years are entitled to a one-year tax exemption and a subsequent two-year 50% tax reduction. FIEs with a working capital of US$10 million and an operational period of ten years in the financial sector can enjoy a one-year tax exemption and a subsequent two-year 50% tax reduction. Sino-foreign joint ventures investing in selected technology areas are also entitled to the same benefits.

---

9 The withholding tax rate is reduced to 7% if the recipient is a company or partnership which holds directly at least 25% of the shares of the company paying the dividends.

10 The withholding rate is reduced to 7% if it is received from a financial institution.

(v) **Profit Distribution and Reinvestment of Profits:** Profit distribution to the foreign partner of an FIE is not subject to withholding tax. To encourage the second cycle of reinvestment of profits in China, companies can apply for up to a 40% refund of taxes paid for reinvested profits. If the reinvestment is in a 100% export oriented company or a technologically advanced area, the reduction can be raised to 100%. This also applies to infrastructure investment in Hainan SEZ and PNDZ.

The above incentives are not particularly attractive when compared to Singapore companies which can enjoy up to ten years of full tax exemption if they qualify for pioneer status in their industries. The five-year tax holiday is not attractive as it allows only two years of full tax exemption. The criteria for Export-Oriented and Technologically Advanced Enterprises to export 70% of total production is not realistic as most FIEs set up production lines in China for the purpose of tapping the Chinese domestic market.

CAPITAL STRUCTURE

Debt Equity Rules

For an enterprise to be classified as an FIE, the share of foreign equity in the company must be at least 25% of the registered capital. In addition, the debt-equity requirements as shown in Table 2-2 must also be met.

Bank Loans and Debt-Equity Ratios

The Bank of China (BOC) and the China International Trust and Investment Corporation (CITIC) have been the major suppliers of loans to foreign-invested enterprises. However in recent years, other banks, such as the Bank of Communications and the Industrial and Commercial Bank of China, have also emerged to compete with more than 75 foreign banks and joint venture banks to vie for the foreign-invested enterprise banking business.

Currently, foreign banks are restricted from lending in Renminbi. Therefore, foreign banks focus on hard currency businesses. These include forex loans, discounting bills, handling foreign trade accounts, remittances, trading foreign shares and bonds and accepting deposits.

TABLE 2-2
Debt/Equity Requirement for Foreign Investment Enterprises in China

Value of Project	Minimum Foreign Capital Requirement	Other Requirements
US$3 million	70%	Nil
US$3–10 million	50%	Not less than US$2.1 million to be invested.
US$10–30 million	40%	Not less than US$5 million to be invested.
Above US$30 million	33.3%	Not less than US$12 million to be invested.

Loans by BOC to joint ventures are governed by the Procedures of the BOC for Loans to Enterprises with Foreign Investment. The measures under the procedures require a joint venture to have its registered capital paid up in full before loan companies are eligible for loans.

In addition, the credit line extended to a foreign-invested enterprise's Renminbi working capital facilities are commonly structured as one-year revolving credit lines with the BOC and other specialised banks. Borrowing arrangements and amount of credit are determined during the joint venture contract negotiations. Although the credit line is normally renewed, the extending of the credit amount is not easy and collateral is required.

Foreign-invested enterprises are allowed to borrow Renminbi working capital funds which are then traded at the swap markets to obtain forex financing. It should be noted that the Chinese authorities generally require all companies to have a positive forex account in business operations.

In March 1987, the Interim Provisions of the State Administration for Industry and Commerce Concerning the Ratio Between Registered Capital and Total Amount of Investment of Chinese-Foreign Equity Joint Ventures were established. The provisions seek to ensure that joint ventures are not highly leveraged.

Under the provisions, when the total investment or contract value is less than US$3 million, the actual contributions of the partners must be at least 70%, that is, only loans up to 30% are allowed. For projects between US$3–10 million, US$10–30 million and above US$30 million, the values of 50%, 40% and 33.33% must be paid-up, respectively. This effectively limits the debt-equity level of investments in China.

If interest is tax deductible, the effective interest paid by a firm is lower than the nominal interest because part of the nominal interest will be paid by the Internal Revenue Service. Therefore, the corporate tax rate will have an impact on the firms' debt equity ratios. If the corporate tax rate for foreign investors is very low, then the effective interest rate will be closer to the nominal rate of interest. Foreign investment in China may not need to have the same debt equity ratios as they have in their home country. Since the corporate tax rates in China are dependent on the location of investment and, hence, different effective rates of interest, we would expect the debt-equity ratio to differ in different parts of China.

CONCLUSION

As the economic reforms in China continue and the affluence of the Chinese increases, China's economy will continue to be a promising market for the immediate future. In addition, the abundance of labour and other resources will provide a competitive edge for companies which are able to find a niche to produce and export to the rest of the world. However, as the tax system is still in a relatively early stage of development, investors have to constantly update their knowledge of the taxation regime to ensure that their competitiveness is not eroded.

REFERENCES

"Business Briefing", *The Economist,* November 1993.

China News Brief, Coopers & Lybrand, Singapore, September 1993.

China Newsletter, Nos. 82, 84 and 85. Price Waterhouse, Hong Kong, 1994.

China Tax Review, Vol. 1, Nos. 1, 3, 4, Hong Kong, 1994.

"China: The Emerging Economic Powerhouse of the 21st Century", *Business Week,* May 1993.

Chou Gilbert, "*China's Tax and Fiscal Reform*". W. I. Carr, Hong Kong, February 1994.

Tan Boon Leng, "Doing Business in China", *The Management Observer* (Singapore), April 1993.

"Tax Matters China", in *Spotlight on Business*, Ernst & Young. Singapore, March 1994.

"The Barbarians at the Gate", *The Economist,* November 1993.

Yang Mu, "Reforming China's Tax System: Problems & Prospects", *IEAPE Background Brief,* No. 60, Singapore, August 1993.

Zweig David, "Reaping Rural Rewards", *The China Business Review,* November–December 1992.

Chapter 3

The Chinese Financial System*

BY
YEO Poh Seng
SIA Siong Huat
TAN Seng Hwee

INTRODUCTION

CHINA'S ECONOMIC GROWTH for the past two years has been in double digit figures. Even though there has been talk about austerity programmes to prevent overheating, the market potential is still tremendous. With the Singapore Government encouraging local companies to invest abroad, particularly in China, it is important that ample research, feasibility studies and planning be conducted.

The objective of this chapter is to present an overview of the banking and financial system in China. The focus will be on the various banking loans available to foreign investors and how such loans affect the choice of investment financing. It should be noted that there are other forms of investment financing apart from banking loans. This includes equity and debt financing for a publicly listed company in the Stock Exchange of Shenzhen and Shanghai. However, this chapter will strictly discuss investment

* We are grateful to Prof. Zeng Kang Ling, Prof. Yang Gan, Ms. Han Ying, Mr. Shang Qi, Mr. Ma Changming and Dr. Cao Yong for providing us with information in accomplishing this mission report.

financing through banking loans from the perspective of a joint local and foreign equity enterprise, a joint local and foreign co-operative enterprise, or a foreign-owned enterprise.

It must be emphasised that China is still undergoing continual reforms and, thus, its policies may be volatile. The information presented here should be used only as a starting point for any potential investor intending to invest in China and funding their business/project through Chinese banking loans. Also, since the procedure and guidelines in banking application may vary from province to province, it is important that clarification be sought with the relevant local authorities.

BACKGROUND INFORMATION

Overview of Banking and Financial Systems in China[1]

Prior to 1978, there was only one bank in China and that was the People's Bank of China. During this time, there was no requirement for a complex, systematic and well-regulated banking system. The People's Bank of China served both as the central bank and commercial bank responsible for all currency, saving and loan transactions.

After 1978, the economic system of China has been changed to a market economy. With this change has come the need for a complete banking and finance structure. The rationale for the reforms in this area include the following:

(i) To establish a strong central bank for macroeconomic management.
(ii) To separate financial policy and business finance in that the former deals with the support of the state-owned bodies while the latter focuses on the commercial sector.
(iii) To establish a uniform, competitive and tightly controlled financial market system, and
(iv) To build a modern financial system.[2]

At the present time, all credit control must be approved by the

---

1 Extracted from China Banking and Financial Regulations.

2 Extracted from the presentation, "Reform of the Financial System in China and Its Relevance to Foreign Investment in China" by Prof. Zeng Kang Ling of South-western University of Finance and Economics on 13 June 1994.

headquarters of the People's Bank of China with the branches serving a monitoring and controlling function. Foreign exchange is now unified to aid the management of foreign exchange transactions, especially for foreign investors.

As shown in Figure 3-1, the People's Bank of China is the central bank and it is responsible for the management of the financial system. The policy banks (i.e., the Industrial and Commercial Bank, Agricultural Development Bank, Bank of China and People's Construction Bank) handle the financing needs of their own respective economic sectors. The Industrial and Commercial Bank provides industrial/commercial loans and collects saving deposits at the urban areas. The Agricultural Development Bank focuses on loans to the agricultural sector. The Bank of China handles all foreign exchange dealings and import/export activities. The People's Construction Bank caters to the financing needs of the real estate sector.

Other banks, like the Bank of Communications, Investment Bank and other regional banks undertake loans, guarantees, insurance, forex dealing and consumer banking services. Unlike the policy banks, these banks have more liberty to set up branches to cater to the market requirements.

The banking regulations specify that banks are not allowed to raise interest rates, directly or indirectly, to attract saving deposits. Loans are categorised into fixed asset loans and working capital loans. Fixed asset loans may only be granted for the construction of infrastructure projects and for high technology investment. Interest rates on this type of loan are fixed.

The working capital loans may be granted for manufacturing, distribution activities and other routine operations of the business. These loans can take the form of short-term loans, overdrafts and credit lines. The term of such loans typically varies from six months to a year and floating interest rates are allowed within the limit set by the central bank. These loans may be denominated in local or foreign currencies.

Forms of Foreign Investment

Foreign investment in China has expanded rapidly since 1979 when foreign investors first came to set up Sino-foreign joint ventures. For example, within Chengdu city the number of Sino-foreign joint ventures has more than tripled from 572 in 1991 to 1,910 in 1993.[3]

FIGURE 3-1
The Organisation of the Banking and Financial Systems of China

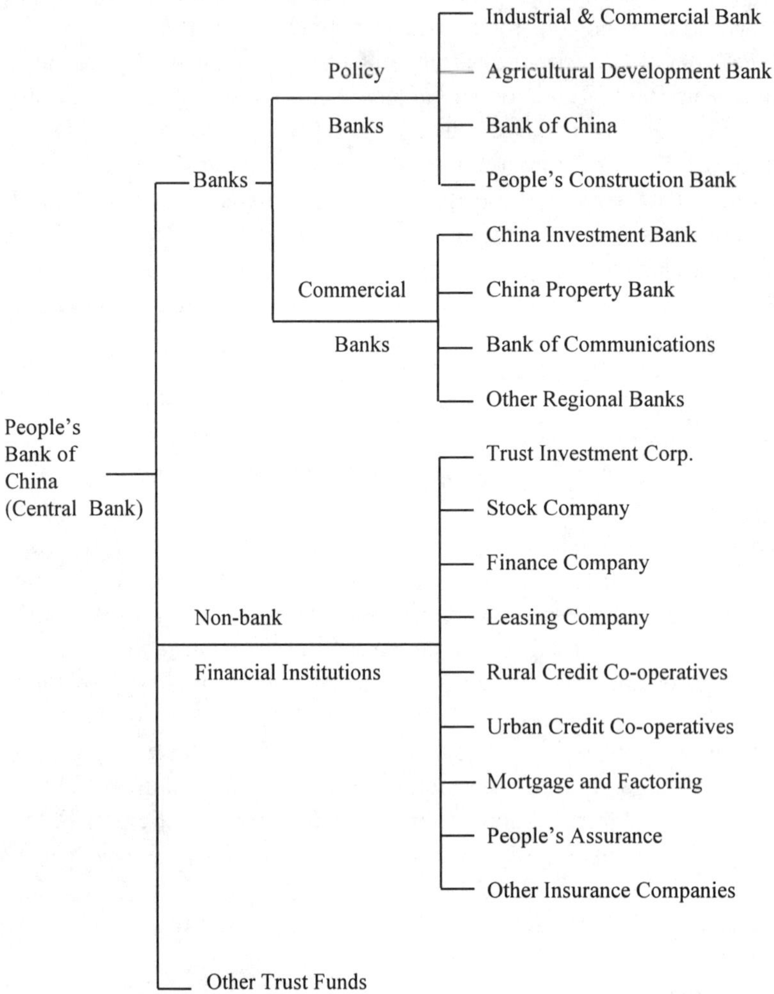

---

[3] Extracted from the presentation, "The Current Situation of Foreign Investment in Sichuan Province" by Prof. Yang Gang, Director of Institute of Economic Reform, the Sichuan Academy of Social Sciences, on 13 June 1994.

Table 3-1 shows the direct investment in China by types (contract basis).[4] There are five common options for foreign investors in China as highlighted in Table 3-1. Each form of investment has its own governing laws, advantages and disadvantages.

TABLE 3-1
Direct Investment in China by Types (Contract Basis)

Type of Investment	1990		1991	
	Number	Value (US$m)	Number	Value (US$m)
Direct Foreign Investment	7,273	6,596.11	12,978	11,976.82
Equity Joint Venture	4,091	2,703.95	8,395	6,080.05
Contractual Joint Ventures	1,317	1,254.10	1,778	2,137.83
Wholly Foreign-owned Companies	1,860	2,443.81	2,795	3,666.95
Joint Exploration	5	194.25	10	91.99

(i) **Direct Foreign Investment:** This takes the form of direct purchases of equity, real estate, stocks, bonds and etc. As shown in Table 3-1, it forms up to 50% of the total foreign investment in China. This is the most economically viable type in the context of China where the possibility of contractual difficulties makes it especially costly to coordinate economic activities via arm's length transactions in the marketplace.

(ii) **Equity Joint Ventures:** Sino-foreign equity joint ventures have been the most popular form of foreign investment in China. In 1991, a total of 8,395 equity joint ventures were established in China with a total value of US$6,080 million.

The law concerning equity joint ventures is the most developed of all China's foreign investment laws. It is the most regulated and defined law among all foreign investment vehicles and, thus, the most attractive. Usually a limited liability corporation is formed with the Chinese contributing land, factory or some machinery, materials, or labour. The foreign partner is expected to provide

---

4 Extracted from "Foreign Investment in the PRC, 1991–92", *Jetro China Newsletter,* No. 102, January–February 1993, pp. 16–21.

technology, capital equipment, external marketing expertise, management, and additional working capital. Earnings are distributed according to equity shares (certificates rather than shares of stock).

There are four basic requirements to establish equity joint ventures which include supplying advanced technical equipment and scientific management methods; enhancing technical development; developing the export of products; and training technical and managerial personnel. The duration of a joint venture is almost limitless, ranging from 10 years to 30 years or more. It is possible not to prescribe a contract period in the contract.

(iii) **Contractual Joint Ventures:** In 1988, China enacted the Law on Chinese-Foreign Contractual Joint Ventures. Table 3-1 indicates that a total of 1,778 contractual joint ventures (CJV) were established in the People's Republic of China (PRC) in 1991. In establishing a CJV, the Chinese and foreign parties must prescribe in the contract such matters as the investment or conditions for co-operation, the distribution of earnings or products, the sharing of risk and losses, the manner of operation and management, and the ownership of the property when the CJV is terminated. This differs from Equity Joint Ventures in that funds, equipment, materials, and services provided by the partners are not considered equities but are repaid at a set rate of return. Most CJVs are found in the service, tourist, construction and other small industries. They are also frequently utilised for large investment projects involving the development of natural resources.

(iv) **Foreign Capital Enterprises:** In 1986 and 1990, the law and its rules for implementation, on enterprises operated exclusively with foreign capital was separately promulgated. This law attempted to clarify the legal position of wholly foreign-owned (WFO) enterprises. The number of WFO enterprises reached 2,795 by 1991. Foreign Capital enterprises refer to those enterprises established in China by foreign investors exclusively with their own capital. WFO enterprises are usually allowed greater independence in business planning and management. The main advantage is freedom in business decision-making from PRC management.

The 1986 Law sets forth three criteria for the establishment of a WFO enterprise which include benefits to China's national economy, high technology and the export of all or most of its products. The law requires a WFO enterprise to determine its duration at the time of application which can be extended upon approval by the competent authority. This indicates that China does not intend to limit the duration of WFO enterprises. Some limitations on the types of business activities accorded WFO status include the press, publishing, television, movies, domestic commerce and insurance.

Availability of Banking Loans

Loans may be granted by local policy banks or foreign banks. Each bank operates within the rules and regulations of the People's Bank of China, the central bank. However, each bank has its own degree of flexibility in structuring loans. It is most convenient for foreign investors to apply for loans from the Bank of China, especially in the inland cities where foreign bank representation is totally absent.[5]

Types of Loans[6]

The Bank of China handles the following types of loans:

(i) **Fixed Assets Loan:**[7] A fixed asset loan is typically granted to finance construction costs, purchase of technology and equipment, and installation costs in connection with capital construction and technological transformation projects. It takes the following forms:
  (a) Short and medium-term loan.
  (b) Buyer's credit.
  (c) Syndicated loan.
  (d) Project financing.

  The term of a fixed asset loan shall not exceed seven years. However, it can be extended for some special projects subject to the approval of the Bank of China provided that such an extension shall end one year before the expiration of the business licence of the

---

5 As informed by Ms. Han Ying, deputy director of Sichuan Service Centre for Enterprises with Foreign Investment.

6 Extracted and translated from *Investment Guide to Zhuhai, Special Economic Zone* by Foreign Investment Services Centre of Zhuhai, May 1990.

7 Extracted and translated from *Reform of the Financial System in China and its Relevance to Foreign Investment in China* by Prof. Zeng Kang Ling of Southwestern University of Finance and Economics on 13 June 1994. To obtain this type of loan is very difficult with the current tight credit control exercised by the Central Bank.

enterprise.

(ii) **Working Capital Loans:** Working capital is granted to meet the funds requirement of enterprises in the process of their manufacturing and marketing of products and normal operations. The term of a working capital loan shall not exceed 12 months and it takes the following forms:
   (a) Production reserves and revolving funds.
   (b) Temporary credit.
   (c) Overdraft on current account.

(iii) **Renminbi Loans Against Mortgage:** This is handled by the Bank of China according to provisional measures, for the borrowing of Renminbi loans mortgaged with foreign currencies by enterprises with foreign investment, promulgated by the People's Bank of China. For Renminbi loans, the interest rate for the state-owned enterprises regulated by the People's Bank of China is applicable. For foreign currency loans, the interest rate is either the consolidated interest rate set by the Bank of China or the rate agreed upon between the lender and borrower in the light of international market conditions. In the event that foreign buyer's credit or other credit facilities are involved, the interest rate is specified in the related agreement plus a margin.

(iv) **Stand-by Credit:** This is given by the Bank of China after it reviews and approves of the application by enterprises for special standby purposes.

Loans can be provided in local (i.e., denominated in Renminbi) and foreign currencies denominated in either U.S. dollars, pound sterling, Japanese yen, Hong Kong dollars, Deutsche mark or other convertible currencies acceptable to the Bank of China. For Renminbi loans, the interest bearing period is fixed and the interest is calculated according to the regulations of the People's Bank of China. For foreign currency loans, the same conditions are effected in accordance with the relevant provisions of the loan agreement.

Pre-requisites for Granting of Loans

The foreign investment must satisfy the following criteria:

(i) Obtain a business licence issued by the Administration for Industry and Commerce of the People's Republic of China and open account(s) with the Bank of China.

(ii) Registered capital must be fully paid at the specified time which has been certified according to relevant regulations.

(iii) The resolution on and power of attorney for the borrowing by its board of directors has been determined.

(iv) The capital construction project has been approved by the planning authorities.

(v) It has the ability to repay the loan and can provide reliable security(ies) for repayment of the principal and interest.

Procedures in the Application of a Loan

The following procedures must be satisfied when applying for loans:

(i) The enterprise must file an application to the Bank of China with relevant certificates and documents as the case may require.

(ii) The Bank of China will investigate the information provided with the loan. Both parties will sign the loan agreement once it is approved.

(iii) The enterprise must use the funds obtained from the loan according to the time, amount and usage specified in the loan agreement.

(iv) When an enterprise applies for a loan from the Bank of China, it must provide security(ies) acceptable to the Bank of China, if so required. These securities may be in the form of:

 (a) Letter of Guarantee. This is issued by a financial institution in view of good credit standing and debt service capability in repayment of the principal and interest of the loan.

 (b) Mortgage. An enterprise may mortgage its properties, rights and interest to the Bank of China as securities for repayment of the principal and interest of the loan. The collateral may be:

  (i) house property, machinery and equipment.

  (ii) marketable goods in stock.

  (iii) deposits or certificates of deposit in terms of foreign currencies.

  (iv) negotiable securities and bills.

  (v) equity shares and other transferable rights and interests.

FINDINGS OF BUSINESS MISSION

The Business Mission presented opportunities to obtain the views of government officials, academicians, and industrialists on the availability of banking loans to foreign investors. The factors that influence the availability of banking loans can be summarised as follows:

(i) The Chinese economy is currently in an overheated state and government efforts are underway to cool the economy through curbing the money supply and thereby controlling inflation. As an illustration, approximately 200 billion Renminbi are presently loaned out, and the annual interest rate varies from 12 to 15%. Although this is a cyclical feature of the economy, the effort to tighten credit at the central bank level decreases the availability of funds that could be channelled into loans to industries. The government's macroeconomic policy has therefore made it difficult for industries to obtain loans at present.

(ii) Local government officials and industrialists expressed the view that part of the objective of having joint ventures with foreigners was to obtain foreign funds for the projects. It was therefore expected that foreign partners should contribute a fair share of the total project cost and not to expect to raise loans in China. In fact, incentives such as tax holidays and the opening of the Chinese domestic market to goods produced by foreign joint ventures in China were aimed at attracting foreign funding of joint ventures.

(iii) The current financial system in China is backward when compared with those of western economies. Financial services are not really available, funds are difficult to obtain and the financial markets are just starting to take shape in the coastal cities, most notably in Shanghai. Furthermore, there is no access to information on how the products of Chinese banks fare in comparison with those of foreign banks. Chinese banking industry personnel are unfamiliar with the common operational procedures of banks practised elsewhere in the world. All of these factors contribute to the lack of financial instruments that banks could use to meet the funding needs of industries.

(iv) The absence of foreign banks in the inland cities such as Chengdu and Chongqing makes it difficult for foreign joint venture companies to obtain foreign currency denominated loans from these banks. At present, foreign banks are only allowed to operate in the coastal cities such as Shanghai and Xiamen. Even if arrangements could be made to tap the funds from the foreign banks in the coastal cities, government restrictions on the foreign banks do not permit them to deal in Renminbi. Also, loan limits of 30% of the paid-up capital of joint ventures add to the scarcity of loans.

(v) Currently, fixed assets loans are not easily granted unless they pertain to the construction of infrastructure and high technology investment. The main infrastructure construction is currently centred on power generation, highways and railways construction projects. High technology investments include semiconductor manufacturing, electronics and computer industries.

(vi) The security and debt financing market is highly underdeveloped. The Shanghai Securities Exchange and the Shenzhen Stock Exchange are the only two official stock exchanges in China. In 1992, the Chinese government started to issue a new type of stock (B shares) targeted at international investors and structured in accordance with the international standards. However, the B shares carry considerable risks. The companies are under-researched and they are audited using local accounting procedures rather than globally accepted international accounting standards. The B shares are also illiquid, under-legislated and expensive. It will therefore take time for the capital market to develop in a more sophisticated manner.

(vii) Many Chinese state-owned enterprises are incurring losses, are technologically ineffective, and suffer from low productivity and poor quality outputs. With the present tight credit controls by the central bank, it is difficult for these state-owned enterprises to obtain bank loans to upgrade their operations. Therefore, the top priority for these enterprises is to obtain funds, management skills and the right technology from foreign partners.[8]

INVESTMENT FINANCING STRATEGY

It is very important to perform a feasibility study and project the cash flow for the whole project so that capital adequacy can be planned in

[8] From the discussion with Mr. Yang Ting Wei, Director of Mianyang City Development Council, Mr. Yun Zheng Xin, Deputy Chief Engineer of Ya Guang Electronic Engineering Factory, and Mr. Cheng Rong Wei, Vice General Manager, Star Enterprise Corporation.

advance to avoid unnecessary business failure, or the need to raise loans from local Chinese banks. The investment should be in different phases and all potential cash flows should be accounted for in the business venture. One recommended strategy would be to commence operations with the least possible paid-up capital and plow back any future profits from the operations for further expansion.[9] In the long-term, the company could plan to list themselves in the local or foreign stock exchanges so that another form of funds could be tapped in raising capital.

Currently, machinery and technology may be capitalised up to a maximum of 20% of the paid-up capital. Therefore, a foreign investor should capitalise on this provision to reduce the cash outlay and the risks involved in the investment. Another strategy for foreign investors to consider is to acquire those state-owned enterprises in financial distress at good bargain prices as an initial step in establishing business operations.

With the present tight credit policy by the central bank, loans may not be accessible in China. In situations where funding is really needed, one strategy might be to raise the funds outside of China and then engage in foreign currency to Renminbi swap. This swap arrangement allows a foreign investor to hedge their price risk, attributed to changing foreign exchange rates, when they need to repay their borrowings from the business profits denominated in Renminbi. Lastly, *guanxi* relationships (if any) should be optimised to raise funds under special provisions by the local authorities.

CONCLUSION

Foreign investors can choose to use direct foreign investments, equity joint ventures, co-operative joint ventures, wholly owned subsidiary or joint exploration, as forms of investment. Banking loans in China have been classified as fixed asset loans, working capital loans, Renminbi loans against mortgages and, standby credit.

Currently, the Chinese government is curbing the money supply to control inflation. Therefore, banking loans are not easily accessible to foreign investors and, therefore, they should consider the whole proj-

---

9 As recommended by Prof. Yang Kang, Director of Institute of Economic Reform, the Sichuan Academy of Social Sciences.

ect/business cash flow requirements and not expect to raise loans in China.

We strongly recommend that a feasibility study be conducted with all cash flows projected *a priori*. Since the apparent inaccessibility of banking loans to foreign investors increases the riskiness of the project, we recommend a strategy of setting up the initial venture with the least possible paid-up capital. Future earnings may then be used for further expansion.

REFERENCES

China Economic Digest, Summer Issue 1993, pp. 42–3, 48–9, 66–7.

"China's Markets Take Shape", *Euromoney, A Supplement to Euromoney,* June 1992.

"Foreign Investment in the PRC", *Jetro China Newsletter,* No. 102, January–February 1993, pp. 16–21.

"Foreign Investors Eye China's Vast Interior", *The Straits Times* (Singapore), 15 February 1994.

Guide to Investment of Chongqing Economic and Technological Development Zone, Chongqing Economic and Technological Development Zone, 1993.

Kaufman George G., *Banking Structures in Major Countries*, Kluwer Academic Publishers, Boston, 1992, pp. 113–54.

Levin Mike, "China Investment's a Two-way Street", *Global Finance,* February 1993, pp. 46–7.

Linn Gene, "Getting it Right Second Time", *Asian Business,* November 1993, pp. 42–53.

"Singapore Firm Give South China a Miss", *The Straits Times,* 15 February 1994.

"SM: Look at the Bottomline When Planning", *The Straits Times,* 12 July 1993.

"Wuhan's State Firms Face Bleak Times", *The Straits Times,* 6 May 1994.

Chapter 4

The Availability of Banking Loans to Foreign Investors in China and the Strategy of Investment Financing

BY
CUI Wei
David LEE Seng Quee
SEET Yeng Fang

INTRODUCTION

WITH THE PUSH towards regionalisation by the Singapore government and the opening up of China's economy, it is inevitable that many investors are targeting China. Hence, it is timely to discuss the availability of bank loans to foreign investors in China and the strategy of investment financing. The potential of the Chinese market is a great attraction for foreign investments. Furthermore, the Chinese government is giving tax incentives to foreign investors. At home, the government is also encouraging local businessmen to invest in China and providing incentives and assistance to help them set up operations.

THE FORM OF FOREIGN INVESTMENT

In discussing the availability of bank loans for foreign investors in China, it is appropriate to begin with the forms of foreign investments available in China since bank loans will inevitably be taken in the name of the investment vehicle.

Direct foreign investment generally fall into three major categories, namely joint venture enterprises, contractual business co-operations and wholly-owned foreign enterprises.

Joint Venture Enterprise or Corporation

This is a sino-foreign equity joint venture, which results in the formation of a Chinese legal person. The formation of and other regulations relating to the equity joint venture are governed by the Law of the People's Republic of China on Sino-Foreign Joint Ventures ("Equity Joint Venture Law") and their Implementing Regulations.

Contractual Business Co-operation

The contractual or co-operative joint venture may or may not result in the formation of a Chinese legal entity, as the joint venture partners so choose. Co-operative joint ventures are regulated by the Sino-Foreign Contractual Joint Venture Law of the People's Republic of China.

Enterprises with 100% Foreign-Owned Capital

The wholly foreign-owned enterprise is operated in China exclusively with foreign capital but it is registered in China as a Chinese legal person. This form of investment is governed by the Law of the People's Republic of China on Enterprises Operated Exclusively with Foreign Capital.

It is important that the form of foreign investment be considered carefully as different forms will impact the availability of banking loans and the strategy of investment financing.

THE VITAL FACTORS FOR OBTAINING BANK LOANS IN CHINA

In considering the availability of bank loans to foreign investors in China, apart from the creditworthiness or credit rating of the foreign investor in the international financial circle, the following factors have to be taken into consideration:

(i) The type of industry;
(ii) The location of the investment; and
(iii) The collateral available to secure the bank loans.

Type of Industry

China has established special economic zones, economic technological development zones and open coastal cities; and has designated the eastern coastal region as the area where special legislative and economic benefits will be given to encourage foreign investment in these specific targeted areas. In general, foreign investments are encouraged and given priority in the following areas:

(i) Industries that bring in foreign currency;
(ii) Industries that utilise domestic resources, including labour and raw materials;
(iii) Export oriented manufacturing industries;
(iv) Technology transfer projects;
(v) Infrastructural development projects; and
(vi) Agriculture and forestry.

In line with the Chinese Government's policy of encouraging foreign investment, the financing of such investments may be available from the three new policy-lending Chinese banks — the National Development Bank, the Import and Export Credit Bank and the Agricultural Development Bank. At present, only the National Development Bank and the Import and Export Credit Bank have been established.

It has been estimated that improperly secured loans made by the Chinese policy-lending banks amounted to about 200 billion RMB Yuan. As a result of these actions, Vice-Premier Zhu Rongji issued a directive for these loans to be recalled by September 1993. However, by August 1993, the Chinese banks could only retrieve about 72.7 billion Yuan — about one-third of these improperly secured loans. Consequently, the deadline was extended from September to 31 December 1993 and was then further extended to April 1994. This credit squeeze may cause difficulty for funding of investment projects.

Location of Investment

The location of the investment is also a vital factor in the determination of the availability of bank loans to foreign investors. For example, if the investment is in a remote location where only a small provincial bank is in operation, a bank loan may be difficult to obtain as compared to an investment located in one of the special economic zones, economic technological zones or major cities, where not only the major Chinese banks but also the joint venture banks and branches of foreign banks are located.

Land Ownership and Rights to Use Land

The Constitution provides that land can be owned either by the state (the people) or by collectives. Ownership is defined under Article 71 of the *General Principles of the Civil Law* as "The owner's right in accordance with law to possess, use, benefit from and dispose of his own property." After the amendment of Article 10 of the Constitution in 1988, several pieces of legislation were passed to implement the granting and assignment of leaseholds in the land.

Article 8 provides that the term "grant of a leasehold" refers to the act by which the State, in its capacity as landowner, grants the right to use land for a fixed term in years to a user of land, and the user of land pays to the State a sum for the grant of the leasehold. When a leasehold is granted, the parties shall enter into a grant contract. This indicates that while creating "leasehold interests", these interests also are contractual in nature.

A foreign-invested enterprise which has acquired land use rights will be permitted to use the land only in the manner approved. Where a project is approved by the state which requires land for its implementation, the approval carries with it an agreement to allow use of the land necessary to implement the project. Approval can only be granted by the People's Government above the county level.

Rights to use the land are personal. Transfer, lease and inheritance of land use rights and the right to profit from the deal with appurtenance to the land are restricted in accordance with the provisions of the *Law of Land Administration*. However in specific areas as Tianjin, Shanghai, Shenzhen and Guangdong land rights are obtained through competitive bidding or auction with negotiated tenure and contained in the contract for the transfer of the right to use that land. This type of consignment contract usually relates to specific parcels of land in special economic development zones or technological development zones. Normally the restrictions are that the land must be developed before any dealing is permitted with the land use right. The holder of the right to use can deal with the right in any lawful way which includes mortgage of the right, transfer and gift. This right is also inheritable. Any dealing with the structures on the land and the right to use land must be registered with the responsible government agency with the required fee payable.

Therefore, depending upon the location of the investment, in certain areas, the holder of land rights to use can deal with the right to use which includes mortgage of the right. In other words, in certain areas, the joint venture may be able to acquire a mortgageable right to use land rather than merely a contractual right of use for a specific purpose as approved.

STRATEGY FOR INVESTMENT FINANCING

In formulating a strategy for investment financing, an understanding and consideration of the following factors are necessary:

(i) Banking system and reforms in China;
(ii) Exchange control regulations;
(iii) Interest differential between domestic financing and off-shore financing;
(iv) Availability of swap facilities; and
(v) In the case of off-shore financing, sources of foreign currency for the repayment of principal and interest of bank loans.

Banking System and Reforms

Reform of the financial system began in the 1980s in parallel with the country's overall economic reform programme. During the pre-reform days, banks in China were acting as mere cashiers and allocating funds in strict accordance with state plans.

The People's Bank of China (PBOC) controlled all retail banking. The four specialised banks, namely Bank of China, People's Construction Bank of China, Agricultural Bank of China and the Industrial and Commercial Bank of China, which account for 85% of bank assets were, in effect, government departments. For example, the Industrial and Commercial Bank of China (ICBOC) with 30,000 branches and 500,000 employees, had 30% of its loans made for reasons of "policy" — to prop up loss-making and uncreditworthy state-owned industrial firms.

It was almost impossible for the central bank to control the money supply since the branches of the central bank and specialised banks were treated as administrative units of the government and local officials have considerable power to ignore orders from the central bank to regulate money supply. One of the most important reforms in the banking industry is that the allocation of funds is no longer planned by the central bank. The PBOC has also changed its policy on banking supervision whereby direct intervention on banking operations is augmented by introducing new financial and legal measures to regulate the industry.

Presently, the four specialised banks are being re-structured into commercial banks. Their current "policy" lending business will be separated and transferred to the three policy-lending banks which are being formed — the National Development Bank, the Import and Export Credit Bank and the Agricultural Development Bank. These three new policy-lending banks will primarily offer loans to key state projects, the export of capital goods and the long term development of agriculture goods. On the other hand, the four specialised banks operate as commercial banks which are solely responsible for their own profits, losses and business risks.

There are plans to turn the People's Bank of China into a fully functional central bank under the supervision of the State Council. The PBOC will formulate and carry out independent monetary policy such as interest rate policy and bond trading to adjust the money supply rather than adopting measures to control the lending and loan purposes of the Chinese banks.

The participation of foreign banks and the opening up to foreign investment opportunities are important components of the ongoing reforms of the banking system. Representative offices and branches continue to proliferate in the major cities. More joint venture banks are being approved. However, the government still limits the setting up of branches by foreign banks to the coastal regions. For example, Hongkong Bank's recent bid to upgrade its Wuhan representative office to a branch was shelved by the PBOC. A list of joint venture banks, branches and representative offices in major parts of China is given in Appendix 4-1.

Foreign banks are allowed to make foreign exchange loans to foreign joint ventures. However, these foreign banks generally are not permitted to make foreign exchange loans to Chinese companies, take domestic currency deposits or make domestic currency loans. According to Coopers & Lybrand's *China News Brief* (April 1994), China has gradually allowed foreign banks to conduct transactions in Yuan on a trial basis in selected localities such as Xiamen, Pudong of Shanghai municipality and Guangdong. Foreign banks will initially be allowed to handle Renminbi business related to foreign invested enterprises and gradually those related to state enterprises but they will still be prohibited from taking Renminbi deposits. Foreign-invested enterprises are allowed to borrow foreign currency funds from domestic banks or directly from abroad according to the needs of their operations.

Under the 1987 Bank of China Regulation on Providing Loans to Foreign Investment Enterprises, the Bank of China provides loans to foreign-invested enterprises for their construction and business operations with top priority to those export-oriented enterprises that are more efficient export and high-tech enterprises. In order to meet the needs of production and business operations, foreign-invested enterprises can borrow directly from banks or enterprises abroad without the prior approval of State Administration of Exchange Control (SAEC). However, the borrower must report to the exchange control department for recording and registration. A copy of the loan agreement must be registered with the local SAEC within 15 days after the date of signing and have the loan duly registered. The foreign currency borrowed from abroad must be remitted into their foreign currency account inside China.

Exchange Controls

China's recent foreign exchange control policies have as their major objective the curbing of an increasing high inflation rate. With the issue of the Notice of the State Council Concerning Strengthening Control Over The Taking Out and Use of International Commercial Loans on 12 January 1989, there are only ten organisations in the People's Republic of China which have the capacity to engage relatively freely in foreign exchange dealings. Other organisations are restricted by rules applied by the Bank of China on a loan-to-loan basis. Implementation rules issued by the SAEC further enforce strict control over foreign exchange. The foreign exchange regulations state that loans to Chinese entities from foreign banks and companies must be approved under the State Mandatory Plan and must be submitted for examination by the SAEC and the Ministry of Foreign Economic Relations and Trade. Joint ventures may seek working capital loans, loans for the settlement of accounts and fixed asset loans in Renminbi or foreign exchange from the Bank of China. Such borrowings must be reported to the SAEC for recording. Currency remitted in foreign exchange should be used to pay for imported materials, the repayment of principal and interest on loans in foreign exchange, etc.

The principal features of the foreign exchange control laws covered under the Interim Regulations on Foreign Exchange Control of the PRC, the Detailed Rules for the Implementation of Foreign Exchange Controls Relating to Enterprises Using Overseas Chinese Capital, and Enterprises Using Foreign Capital and Joint Ventures Using Chinese Foreign Capital are as follows:

(i) A foreign venture shall apply for and obtain permission from the State Administration of Exchange Control before it can establish a foreign deposit account with an overseas bank;
(ii) Foreign-invested enterprises are required to maintain a balance between foreign exchange receipts and expenses. Expenses, including payment of loans in foreign exchange, may be drawn from foreign deposit accounts or remitted abroad. A foreign business must, therefore, have the ability to earn foreign exchange by exporting a portion of its products; and
(iii) Foreign-invested enterprises are required to remit into China, foreign exchange earned by export products and deposit it in foreign exchange accounts and generally go through procedures of accounting and verification.

Interest Differential

The interest rate for loans in Renminbi ranges from 12 to 14% whereas for loans in foreign currency, say US$, the rate for a six month roll-over is about 5%. Therefore, where available, foreign currency loans with lower interest rates should be pursued. This is especially true where the foreign-invested enterprise has income dominated in the same foreign currency as the borrowed funds.

SWAP Facilities Available

The foreign exchange swap centre was started in 1980, and at present there are over 100 such swap centres across China. The National Foreign Exchange Swap Centre is located in Beijing. SAEC has formulated the Guidelines for the Use of Swapped Foreign Exchange which included:

(i) repayment of overdue foreign loans plus interest that are registered with the SAEC or its branch; and
(ii) repayment of overdue foreign loans and payment of lease fees when the export of the debtor's products are disallowed.

Sources of Foreign Currency for Repayment

Where the foreign-invested enterprise exports its products and has its income dominated in foreign currency, the availability of foreign exchange for repayment of foreign currency loans will not be a problem. However, in the case where the foreign-invested enterprise supplies its products locally (e.g., an infrastructural project supplying power to the community), approval should be obtained for settlement and payment in foreign currency. Where a foreign-invested enterprise is unable to balance foreign exchange receipts and expenses, foreign exchange control regulations provide that accounts may be settled and paid in foreign exchange for products sold domestically if the following criteria are met:

(i) Subject to approval from the foreign trade departments of the government, accounts may be settled in foreign currency for products needed by China which are sold to Chinese institutions engaged in foreign trade so as to replace imports with these products;
(ii) Accounts for commodities in short supply on China's domestic market that are sold to Chinese purchasing institutions may be settled in foreign currency;
(iii) Products sold to Chinese institutions which are manufactured by foreign-invested enterprises with advanced technology and equipment may be settled in foreign currency; and
(iv) Products of foreign-invested enterprises sold in special economic zones and those products purchased by one foreign-invested enterprise from another foreign-invested enterprise may be settled in foreign currency.

THE STRATEGY

The credit squeeze in 1993 may lead to difficulties in funding investment projects. Simultaneously, as a result of the hedging against high risks for China-bound loans, foreign banks are raising interest rates. It is expected that, all things being equal, the foreign investor will source for investment financing on the basis of minimum costs. Due to the interest differential between Renminbi loans and foreign currency loans (there is no restriction on a foreign-invested enterprise borrowing either domestically or abroad in foreign currency), the foreign investor should opt for foreign currency bank loans under the following circumstances:

(i) Where the foreign-invested enterprise has foreign exchange income either through exports or approved settlement arrangements;

(ii) Its investment is located in one of the special economic development zones or technological development zones in either Tianjin, Shanghai, Shenzhen and Guangdong, where the rights to use land are not mere contractual rights for a specific approved purpose but can be dealt with including mortgage;

(iii) In the case of domestic loans in foreign currency, the land use rights held by the joint venture can be mortgaged as security to the Chinese bank. However, it is to be noted that under the 1987 regulations, the Bank of China can extend term loans not exceeding seven years and working capital loans not exceeding 12 months. Also, other fees charged by the Bank of China vary on a case by case basis. It is appropriate to mention here that one of the factors to be considered will also be the ability of the Chinese partner to influence the availability of financing by the Chinese banks;

(iv) In the event that the Chinese bank is not in a position to offer foreign currency loans, the foreign investor should explore the possibility of the Chinese bank taking the land use rights as security by way of a mortgage for a standby letter of credit line which can be established in favour of an off-shore bank for a foreign currency loan;[1]

(v) On the matter of insurable interests of the joint venture's properties,

---

[1] Due to the differential in interest cost, it will be less expensive to borrow foreign currency than to borrow in Renminbi.

the People's Insurance Company of China can provide such insurance cover. International insurance companies (based in Hong Kong) are also prepared to cover insurable interests for the joint venture's properties in China; and

(vi) Due to the lack of legislation covering hire purchase, leasing or factoring, working capital financing is on the basis of short term roll-over loans, especially for foreign currency loans.

CONCLUSION

In conclusion, before investing in China, it is important to decide on the form of the investment vehicle as it will affect the strategy for financing. The availability of banking loans is dependent on the type of industry and the location of the investment. An understanding and knowledge of the land use rights, the banking environment, exchange controls, interest differentials and SWAP facilities will help in planning the most appropriate investment financing strategy.

APPENDIX 4-1

JOINT VENTURE BANKS, BRANCHES AND REPRESENTATIVE OFFICES

Joint Venture Banks, Branches and Representative Offices that have been established include:

Shanghai

International Bank of Paris and Shanghai (JV)
Dresdner Bank of Germany (Branch)
Bangkok Bank of Thailand (Branch)
Daiwa Bank of Japan (Branch)
ANZ Bank of Australia (Branch)
Swiss Bank Corporation (RO)
First National Bank of Boston (RO)
Commerzbank of Germany (RO)
American Express Bank (RO)
N. M. Rothschild & Sons (RO)

Dao Heng Bank of Hong Kong (RO)
Citibank (having relocated its headquarters from Hong Kong)

Tianjin

Credit Lyonnais of France (Branch)
Societe Generale of France (Branch)
Chase Manhattan Bank of America (Branch)

Ningbo, Zhejiang

Zhejiang Commercial Bank (JV)

Xiamen

Xiamen Commercial Bank (JV)
Citibank (RO)

Beijing

Far East Bank of America (RO)
Citibank (RO)

Harbin

Chiyu Bank of Hong Kong (RO)

Guangzhou

Sakura Bank of Japan (Branch)
Citibank (RO)
Nanyang Commercial & Industrial Bank of Hong Kong (Branch)

Dalian

Nanyang Commercial & Industrial Bank of Hong Kong (Branch)

Shenzhen

Chinese Mercantile Bank (JV)
Nanyang Commercial & Industrial Bank of Hong Kong (Branch)

REFERENCES

China — Business Guide Book (English Version), China Intric Limited, 1993.

China News Brief, Coopers & Lybrand, January–April 1994.

Doing Business in Asia, Vol. 1, CCH Asia Limited, 1994.

Investment Guide of Beijing, Chinese Government, September 1993.

Tan Cheng Leong and Terence T. S. Lim, *China Business and Investment Opportunities*, Cassia Business Intelligence Series, 1993.

LOCATION

Chapter 5

The Choice of Relevant Regions in China: Coastal Versus Inner Regions

BY
DENG Feng
Norman SOLIHIN
OI Tian Poon

INTRODUCTION

CHINA'S OPEN DOOR policy has drawn huge foreign investments, which have resulted in rapid economic development over the last 15 years. This rapid economic development has changed the economic structure of China. The early investments were concentrated along the coastal regions and the main rivers across the country. As foreign investments in the coastal regions increased, the cost of doing business has gone up and investment opportunities there have become less attractive. Now, the inner region offers an interesting alternative to investors.

The rich natural resources and abundant semi-skilled labour of the inner regions give enterprising investors an interesting and untapped opportunity. Furthermore, the central government is keen to reduce the income gap between the coastal and the inner regions to prevent social unrest. Peasants from interior regions are already flooding to coastal cities for work causing excess demand for railway service and housing problems. New technology parks have been planned and are being constructed in the inner regions to provide the infrastructure needs of investors. Investors are also offered good concessions and tax holidays for investment in the inner regions. The transportation and infrastructure problems of the inner regions have also been given top priority by the state and provincial governments. Air, land and water transportation facilities have been planned under an integrated transportation master plan.

The main objective of this report is to explore the investment opportunities in the inner regions since the coastal regions are already well-known to foreign investors. Based on subsequent analysis, several suggestions for foreign investors about investment opportunities in the inner regions of China are presented.

THE COMPARISON OF INNER REGION AND COASTAL REGION

When investors look beyond the coastal regions for investment opportunities, they should consider the inner regions like Sichuan province. The central government has chosen it to spearhead economic development in the inner region. Special benefits, a new tax structure, incentives and development assistance have been granted to inner provinces. The governments in the inner provinces are also ready to leverage on new central government policy by offering more important concessions to investors to speed up economic development in line with China's economic liberalisation.

Sichuan province has been targeted to spearhead further economic development in south-west China. It can be zoned into four regions for economic planning. These four regions are:

(i) Chongqing and Chengdu which account for 65% of the foreign investment in Sichuan province;
(ii) The outskirts of Chongqing and Chengdu and the area between these two cities;
(iii) The cities along the Yangtze river's three gorges, such as Fengdu and Fuling; and
(iv) The ethnic minority areas.

The major cities in Sichuan, like Chengdu and Chongqing, were granted equivalent status and privileges to that of the coastal cities in 1992. High priority policies from the central government and local provincial governments provide these cities with tremendous potential to attract foreign investment. Furthermore, the central government's approval to Chengdu and Chongqing of the right to grant investment incentives provides these cities with marketing advantages. For instance, the Chongqing Special Economic Zone along the Yangtze river was granted final approval from the central government in 1993 to have the same privileges as the coastal cities. It has since signed up 166 projects with foreign investors, such as Yamaha Motors of Japan and Motorola Electronics of the U.S.A.

In 1992 and 1993, the total value of foreign investments in Sichuan amounted to US$2.4 billion. Most of these investments were in Chengdu and Chongqing. In 1993 alone, Sichuan attracted 1,910 foreign investment projects which nearly matches the total number of projects signed since the inception of China's economic liberalisation. These buoyant economic activities have helped Sichuan to chalk up an impressive 12.8% economic growth in 1993. The results have been remarkable.

Sichuan's economic success has stimulated economic development in some of the chronically impoverished neighbouring provinces. In 1993, Yunnan province had an economic growth rate of 10%, while Guizhou and Qinhai provinces grew by 9% each. Thus, investors should consider the inner region for their investment more seriously. The following discussion explores these opportunities in more detail.

DOMESTIC MARKET

The inner regions are densely populated. The total population of south-west China is about 230 million, equal to the entire U.S. Sichuan province itself has approximately 110 million people. Furthermore, Sino-foreign joint ventures can market up to 100% of their products in the domestic market whereas the coastal region joint ventures have to export 70% of their products.

Although the per capita income of the inner region is lower than that in the coastal region, the difference is not substantial in terms of purchasing power. It is estimated that the consumer purchasing power of the inner region is about 70% that of Shanghai. This provides joint ventures with a huge domestic market for their products. The market potential in the inner region is very substantial.

NATURAL RESOURCES

One very important advantage of the inner regions is the rich natural resources which exist. For instance, Chongqing and its surrounding area provides more than 3,500 varieties of biological resources such as rice, oil crops, economic crops, medicinal herbs, garden plants and some rare plants, as well as livestock, poultry and fresh water fish. Mineral resources like coal, natural gas, iron, strontium, gypsum, limestone, silex and silica are in great abundance. Chongqing has huge hydropower potential; the Yangtze and Jialing Rivers can provide about 400 billion cubic metres of water flow annually. There are 51 more rivers in the Sichuan basin which could be developed to provide hydropower and other needs.

LABOUR SUPPLY

Availability

The inner regions, such as Sichuan province, have large populations. Sichuan province has 110 million people which is more than Mexico's population. Joint ventures in the inner region will be able to utilise this huge labour supply source.

Skills

The policy of "The Third Frontier" in the 1960s propelled the central government to develop the inner regions, like Sichuan, as their heavy industry and military production bases to discourage the risk of U.S.A. and U.S.S.R. military attacks. Since the end of the "Cold War", a large pool of technically skilled workers has been made available to commercial industry. In Chongqing, there are 360,000 trained technical workers.

Sichuan also has technological research support centres in Chengdu. It has 273 research institutes and 19 universities. There are more than 6,000 important research findings at these centres and over 400 new technologies are being patented annually. Investors could use the technological strengths of these centres and adapt them to commercial usage.

Labour wages in the inner regions are lower than that in the coastal regions. In Sichuan, wage rates are about one-third of that in the coastal cities.

LAND

Land prices in the inner regions are much lower than that in the coastal cities because the former is less developed. The land lease for industrial usage in the Chengdu Hi-tech Development Zone and Chongqing Economic Development Zone are 375 yuan and 276 yuan per square metre, respectively. In comparison, the land lease for Shanghai's Minhang Economic and Technological Zone or Guangzhou's Huangpu ETDZ is about 870 to 960 yuan per square metre, respectively.

The leasing terms have also become more liberal. For non-gratuitous land use rights, the lease period can be 70 years depending on the proposed joint ventures. The standard terms for commercial, industrial and residential uses are 40-year, 50-year and 70-year leases, respectively. When these lease terms expire, they can be extended. Within the government granted lease terms, the land use rights can be transferred by means of inheritance, transfer, mortgage, donation and lending.

TRANSPORTATION

The central government has extended its integrated air-land-water transportation network developments into the inner regions. Massive transportation infrastructure projects are under construction.

Air

With the launch of regional airlines, major improvements in air transportation facilities have been implemented. New airports have been built and existing airports have been upgraded under a RMB 1.5 billion project. Access to inner regions like Sichuan has improved tremendously. Chengdu's Shuangliu Airport is the fourth largest in China and

Chongqing's Jiangbei Airport has been upgraded to handle Boeing 747s. Currently, there are daily flights to Hong Kong, twice weekly flights to Bangkok and Singapore and regular flights to New Delhi.

Highways

Inner regions, like Sichuan province, have allocated massive funds for highway development. There are plans to spend RMB 1.13 billion for an integrated land-and-water transportation network. The Chengdu-Chongqing highway reduces travelling time between the two cities from 12 hours to 3 hours and the distance from 505 to 300 kilometres. This project was completed at the end of 1995. Another project, the Chengdu-Mianyang Toll Expressway, is scheduled for completion by 1997.

The national highway project, the Shanghai-Chengdu arterial highway, will run through Chengdu, Chongqing, Wanxian, Guiyang, Nanning and on to a sea port in Beibu Wan (Beihai). In the first phase, 800 kilometres of high-grade main trunk of the arterial highway will be constructed and the later phases will have more than 2,000 kilometres of regional arterial highways built and existing ones upgraded.

Subway

In recent years, rapid economic growth has resulted in traffic congestion in the urban areas all over China. Inner cities like Chengdu and Chongqing are faced with the same problem. To overcome this problem, Chengdu is planning to construct a 12-kilometre subway line in the near future. This US$500 million project is expected to be partly financed by foreign investors. Chongqing is also planning to construct a subway system.

Rail

Rail transportation is one of the cheaper ways to access the inner regions. Huge infrastructure projects are under construction. The RMB 2.6 billion electrification project from Chengdu-Kunming Railway has just commenced and the Chongqing-Daxian Electric Railway commenced operation in 1995. In 1995, the multiple-track Yangpingguan-Chengdu section of the Baoji-Chengdu Railway and the Daxian-Chengdu Railway was also completed.

Shipping

Sichuan's Chongqing is accessible by ship from Shanghai, Nanjing and Wuhan. Vessels of 2,000 dead-weight tons (dwt) can navigate the whole year and ships of 10,000 dwt are capable of making the journey at certain times of the year.

INFRASTRUCTURE

Telecommunication facilities in inner cities like Chongqing and Chengdu are modern and the international connection is serviced by direct dialling. Over 10,000 lines of programme-controlled telephones have been completed in Chongqing. The second phase of the project of 40,000 lines is being installed, making it one of the highest penetrations in telecommunication in China. In Chengdu, 50,000 IDD lines were installed by the end of 1994. However, there is room for further improvement.

The electrical power of the inner regions is sufficiently generated by the hydropower stations and other methods of generation. The Chongqing Economic and Technological Development Zone has recently completed three transformer stations with a total capacity of 400,000 KVA. The Dangui transformer station of 120,000 KVA is under planning. This will result in a double power line system for the Chongqing ETDZ. These infrastructure facilities are much better than the areas in coastal cities like Guangzhou.

REGULATION, TAX AND LOCAL GOVERNMENT SUPPORT

Regulation

After successfully boosting the economy in the coastal regions, the central government is emphasising economic development in the inner regions. This extension of policy is not based on economic considerations only, but also for political reasons. The widening gap of prosperity between the coastal and inner regions could potentially erupt into social unrest. Investors will find that investment regulations in the inner regions are more relaxed.

Tax

The tax benefits in the inner regions are comparable to the coastal cities. Setting up a factory in one of Sichuan's zones enables companies to take advantage of the ready infrastructure and lower taxes. Foreign-funded companies investing in the zones are exempted from local income tax. Chengdu has several promising zones offering preferential investment terms like the High and New Technologies Development Zone, the Chengdu-Singapore Industrial Garden City and Longquan Development Zone.

Local Government Support

In order to promote economic development in the inner regions, better benefits and incentives have to be provided by both the central and provincial governments. Both levels of government have adopted a more flexible set of investment regulations. The local government has adopted a one-stop service centre for all government approved applications. For instance, a foreign investment could start production within one year after the registration of the company. It is not surprising that a US$10 million deal can be approved and finalised in a few days.

FINANCIAL SECTOR

The inner regions' financial sector is less developed as compared to the coastal regions. The ability of companies to access the capital market for funds is limited. To encourage economic development in the inner region, the local government is looking into developing Sichuan as the financial centre of south-west China. There are plans to set up a securities market in Chengdu. The local government has also applied to the central government to relax the restriction for foreign banks to set up operation in the inner regions.

CONCLUSION

From the above analysis, it can be concluded that investors should consider the inner regions more seriously when they are choosing a site for their investments. Inner regions have abundant natural resources which investors can develop into commercially viable products. Business opportunities are better as compared to the coastal regions.

There are some suitable industries for foreign investment in the inner regions. Natural resources-based industries, skilled-labour industries, infrastructure development related industries and consumer product industries can be good investment opportunities for foreign investors at this stage.

Investors could tap the vast natural resources in the inner regions. Food, metal, chemical, and energy related industries are sufficiently supported by local resources. Also, Sichuan has abundant skilled workers and their wages are about one-third that of the coastal cities. The technical skill of the local workers are suitable for electronic, telecommunication, machinery, and automobile industries.

Many huge infrastructure projects are under construction and some are in the planning stages to support the rapid economic development in the inner regions. Hence, there is a big market for infrastructure development support industries like construction, building material, and public utilities. Because the inner regions have very large populations in their cities, the increasing income level of consumers will create a large domestic market. Furthermore, more relaxed regulations allowing foreign investors to sell 100% of their products locally would provide a ready market and a base for them to develop before exporting.

An investor should use Michael Porter's framework to analyse the competitive economic advantages of their ventures before committing their funds. This will help to identify the most suitable industry. For example, enterprising investors who use efficient and innovative production methods will be able to compete with other existing companies more effectively. Furthermore, the governments of the inner regions are willing to grant approval of existing monopoly or oligopoly industries to new investors in order to push economic development forward. So the threat of new entrants is very high.

The abundant natural resources have resulted in lower bargaining power for suppliers. This problem should ease as more industries are set up in the inner region. Also, customer bargaining power is not high. Demand for products has exceeded supply. Selling price is set based on the purchasing power of the consumers who possess limited bargaining power. Hence, the domestic market potential is very promising.

Investing in the inner regions of China is not without problems. But the central and provincial governments are improving the terms and conditions to attract more investors. More infrastructure projects will be introduced to improve the investment environment. The risk and return trade-off provides viable investments in the inner regions of China and foreign investors should not miss out on the excellent opportunities.

REFERENCE

Porter, Michael, *The Competitive Advantage of Nations*, The Free Press, London, 1990.

Chapter 6

Comparative Study of Investment Opportunities in Two Sichuan Cities: Chongqing and Chengdu*

BY

Sarah CHEAH Lai Yin
GOH Hwee Ping
FOO Shar Kee
TAN Cheng Teck

INTRODUCTION

DEVELOPMENTS IN THE People's Republic of China have been very dramatic after she embarked on her open door policy. Many international and multinational corporations from a wide range of industries are beginning to establish their presence in China although their motives may differ from one another. China has implemented an open door policy successfully with the initial development of four Special Economic Zones and moving toward opening 14 coastal cities to foreign investors. The next phase is to open up the inland provinces and cities, and one of the most promising inland provinces for foreign investors is Sichuan province.

This chapter provides a macro level comparative study of the investment climate and opportunities currently available in the two major cities of Sichuan province, Chengdu and

* The authors would like to express their deepest appreciation to Dr. Cao Yong, Dr. Chen Kang and Associate Professor J. J. Williams for their assistance in this project.

Chongqing. The next section provides background information on Chengdu and Chongqing. This is followed by a SWOT analysis of the two cities including some of the more vital statistics for comparative purposes. Next, the paper provides some insights on the investment regulations, foreign investment opportunities, investment risks and uncertainties, and the advantages which Singapore has to offer. The final section presents a summary and tentative conclusion on opportunities in Sichuan province.

PRELIMINARY INVESTIGATIONS

Sichuan Province

Sichuan province is located more than 2,500 kilometres from the coast of China.[1] The province has been chosen by the central government of China as the "Dragonhead" for spreading prosperity from the coast to the interior. The provincial government of Sichuan is attempting to attract foreign investors to its huge potential domestic market of 110 million people.[2] The Sichuan authorities also see foreign investments as a source of capital to improve local infrastructure. One of the key advantages offered by the Sichuan authorities to foreign investors is access to the domestic market. This is due to the demand generated by 110 million consumers. If Sichuan province was a separate country, then it would be the eighth most populous in the world.

Owing to the difficulty in delivering products to the province's remote interior, a larger percentage of the products manufactured by foreign enterprises in Sichuan are permitted to be marketed locally. Sino-foreign ventures in Sichuan can sell up to 100% of their goods produced to the domestic market as opposed to the general rule of 70% for coastal cities. Two-thirds of the foreign investments in Sichuan, especially Sino-foreign joint ventures, are located in Chengdu and Chongqing. The major foreign investors are from Hong Kong, Taiwan, the U.S., Singapore and Japan. Sino-Singaporean joint ventures are doing quite well in Sichuan, particularly in Chengdu, where Singaporean investors ranked sixth, after Hong Kong, Taiwan, the U.S., Macau and Japan. Several multinational companies like Motorola, General Motors, MacDonald's

---

1 *Business China*, 16 May 1994.

2 *Business China*, 16 May 1994.

and Sanyo have already located in Sichuan province.

In our discussion, we will focus specifically on the two major cities of Chengdu and Chongqing which rival each other for foreign investments. Chengdu, the capital city of Sichuan province, is located inland and its landscape is 40% plains and 60% mountains. Chongqing, on the other hand, is the largest economic centre. It is a water and land transportation hub as well as the first port of foreign trade in the south-west region of China. It is strategically located on the upper reaches of the Yangtze River. Owing to its mountainous terrain, it is also known as the mountain city of China. Chongqing has a very strong military industrial base due to its strategic importance in past history. The municipal government of Chongqing has been given power of autonomy in various areas and it reports directly to the central government of China instead of the provincial government of Sichuan. Chongqing has also been earmarked to be the current and future testbed for new economic reforms in China. As far as the provincial government of Sichuan is concerned, both Chengdu and Chongqing are allowed to compete equally for foreign investments in various areas. Although the actual implementation policies may differ in the two cities, major policies still follow the guidelines stipulated by the provincial government of Sichuan.

Compared to coastal cities, the labour force structure in Chengdu and Chongqing are good and cheaper by 33%. The aggregate purchasing power is also high in both Chengdu and Chongqing due to the critical mass of the domestic market. The provincial government of Sichuan is also trying hard to narrow the disparity in tax and incentives between the coastal cities and the Sichuan cities. Moreover, it is attempting to improve the infrastructure of Sichuan cities in order to compete with the coastal cities for foreign investments.

Chengdu

Chengdu enjoys a certain level of privileges as the capital city of Sichuan province compared to the other cities of the province, other than Chongqing. It is the centre of economic and cultural activity and it is the traffic, postal and communication hub of south-west China. Compared to coastal cities, Chengdu has poorer infrastructure and geographical disadvantages. However, the transportation network within Chengdu is relatively more established than other parts of Sichuan province other than Chongqing. The poor condition of the highway between Chengdu and Chongqing has been resolved with the completion of the new Chengdu-Chongqing highway at the end of 1995. The new expressway cuts the distance between the two cities from 505 kilometres to 300 kilometres, thereby reducing the travel time between the two cities from 12 hours to a mere three hours. There is also another a four-lane 90 kilometre Chengdu-Mianyang Toll Expressway scheduled for completion by 1997. Planning for a 12-kilometre subway line in Chengdu has been completed and construction will be completed in 1997. Sichuan province wants to raise half of the US$500 million estimated cost of the project from foreign investors. In 1995, the multiple-track Yangpingguan-Chengdu section of the Baoji-Chengdu Railway and the Daxian-Chengdu Railway was completed. The RMB 2.6 billion electrification project of the Chengdu-Kunming Railway has just commenced. In 1993, the Shuangliu Airport in Chengdu became the fourth largest airport in China in terms of quantity of cargo, mail and passengers. The airport was opened to overseas airlines in December 1993. A RMB 1.5 billion renovation project to update the airport and aviation systems will be completed by 1997. Charter flights are available daily to Hongkong, twice weekly to Bangkok and to Singapore. Regular flights to New Delhi commenced in the later half of 1994.

Although the current financial investment climate in Chengdu is not as favourable as that of Shanghai, it is poised to become the financial centre of the south-west region of China and a securities exchange market will also be established in Chengdu. With its favourable agricultural conditions, Chengdu has a good market potential for agricultural-based products. Chengdu is also rich in industrial raw materials, mineral resources and water. In addition, it has strong industrial foundation in terms of variety of products, availability of sub-contractors and supply industries, particularly electrical, electronics, metallurgy, motor, chemical, pharmaceutical, textile, communications and construction materials. It also boasts of a fairly high quantity of skilled labour, especially in the science and technology areas, and good middle and upper management staff. Manufacturing investments are particularly favoured in Chengdu and certain products which have been discouraged in coastal cities are highly encouraged in Chengdu.[3]

Figure 6-1 shows the distribution of gross output of Chengdu between the industrial and agricultural sectors. Heavy industry accounts for

---

3 *Business China*, 16 May 1994.

the largest portion of gross output followed by light industry. Agriculture comprises only 15% of the gross output.

Chengdu has several promising zones offering preferential investment terms. Two of the more important ones are the High and New Technologies Development Zone and Chengdu-Singapore Industrial Park which are described below.

FIGURE 6-1
Gross Output of Chengdu

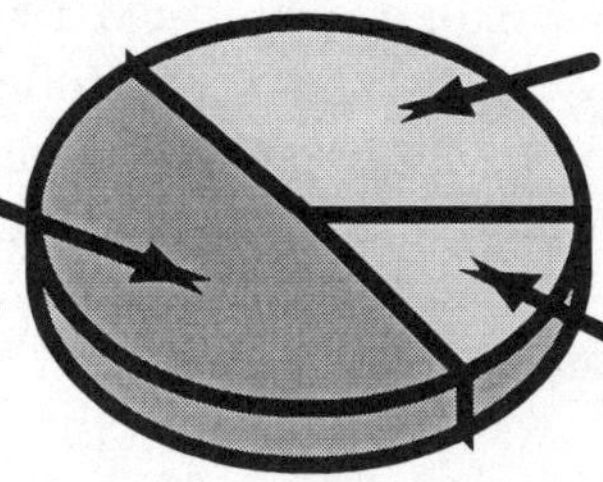

The High and New Technologies Development Zone[4]

This is a state-level zone that focuses on biotechnology, advanced telecommunications, optics-mechatronics integration, new materials and the applications of new technology. The 21.5 square kilometres zone was established in 1989 as an "incubation centre" to grow promising high technologies. It is strategically located near the city centre of Chengdu. Based on its comprehensive advantages, the Chengdu Hi-tech Development zone tries all means to perfect the environment for investment. It was named as one of the ten most advanced science and technology zones in China by the Science Commission of China in 1993. Presently, there are more than 120 companies which have committed US$140 million. There is a predominance of Hong Kong and Taiwan companies although France's Alcatel and Germany's Siemens have also marked their presence.

The major goals of the Chengdu Hi-tech development zone are to

[4] Seminar: A Study of Investment Environment in Chengdu, Sichuan province, June 1994.

commercialise high-tech inventions, to industrialise and to internationalise. The major feature of the Chengdu Hi-tech development zone is its one-stop service. Companies hoping to establish within the zone only require the approval from the management committee of the development zone for any project that costs US$30 million or less. The management committee of the development zone has also been delegated the power of autonomy from the municipal government, thereby enhancing productivity. The corporate tax rate is 15% within the development zone as compared with 33% outside the zone. The tax incentives are similar to the tax recommendations by the central government. This means tax holidays for the first two years in operation and a 50% tax subsidy for the third year in operation. However, the zone suffers from poor communication linkages and power outages. There are only 1,000 IDD lines, although 50,000 have been promised in the near future. Most investors have backup generators to tide them through the current situation until a new 12,000 kw power substation is completed in 1996.

The Chengdu-Singapore Industrial Park[5,6]

This industrial park was set up in 19 May 1993 and the idea was co-initiated by the President of Singapore, Mr. Ong Teng Cheong and the provincial government of Sichuan. It is strategically located in Wuhou district which is geographically between the Shuangliu airport of Chengdu and the city centre of Chengdu and occupies an area of 4.15 square kilometres. It consists of a business and trade district together with a residential district and it is carefully modelled after the Jurong Industrial Estate in Singapore. Currently, there are about 20 companies from Singapore, Hong Kong, Taiwan, the U.S. and Japan which have already made investment commitments in the industrial park. All potential companies must be capital and technologically intensive and non-polluting. The park is due to be completed in five years' time and should have a total of 45 companies with an invested capital of US$200 million by the end of 1996. Investment incentives are awarded on a case-by-case basis. The objective of the park is to achieve a conglomerate of foreign investors so as to establish contacts with foreign countries and to increase the investment interests in the south-west region of China by

---

5 *Business China*, 16 May 1994.

6 Field Trip: Chengdu Hi-Tech Development Zone, June 1994.

providing a more conducive environment for investment. Since Chengdu is the central city in the south-west region of China with a large domestic population, the park has good development potential.

The industrial park also aims to familiarise the investors in the park with the prevailing social, economic and political conditions in China. This will be particularly helpful for Singaporean investors who are typically used to a structured environment. All policies to be implemented for the park will be initiated by the investors with special support from both the governments of China and Singapore. There will be co-operative efforts from both China and Singapore to develop the infrastructure in the park. Dr. John Chen, an NTUC assistant secretary-general, has been made an adviser to the Chengdu municipal government to widen the economic co-operation between Singapore and Chengdu. He has also been appointed as a provincial adviser to a high-powered steering committee in Sichuan to oversee the S$594 million industrial park project. Dr. Chen's role is to help the Chengdu government by introducing Singapore's experience in economic development and urban planning. The steering committee is headed by the Sichuan governor, Xiao Yang, with officials from 18 key government departments. Singapore investments in Chengdu currently amount to US$130 million, making Singapore the fourth largest investing nation in Chengdu, after Hongkong, Taiwan and the U.S.

A Singaporean company, Wearnes Brothers and its joint venture Chinese partner, HuaXin International, have already established themselves in the real estate sector of Chengdu with its property development project of Jinxiu Garden located in the residential district of the industrial park. A representative office of the Chengdu-Singapore Industrial Park has also been established in Singapore. Two projects involving the Singapore Bus Service (SBS) and the NTUC FairPrice were among 194 projects, valued at US$4 billion. They were selected for discussion during the visit of the Chengdu delegation to Singapore, led by Chengdu's party secretary, Mr. Huang YinKui, in May 1994. SBS is keen to team up with a Chinese bus manufacturing company to make luxury coaches while a Chengdu department store is interested in developing a supermarket chain with NTUC FairPrice. Contrary to its name, the industrial park is not earmarked solely for Singaporean investments, although the Singapore Chamber of Commerce is actively recruiting investors.

Chongqing

Chongqing is located geographically to the south-east of Chengdu. It stretches for 208 kilometres from east to west and 220 kilometres from north to south, covering an area of 23,114 kilometres[7]. It experiences a monsoon climate in the mid-subtropical zone with an annual average temperature of about 18 degrees Celsius and an average annual rainfall of 110 cm. These are ideal climatic conditions for agricultural development and account for the city's second ranking amongst Chinese cities in terms of total annual agricultural output.

Chongqing has 9 districts and 12 counties under its jurisdiction. It is very rich in natural resources, boasting of more than 3,500 varieties ranging from biological resources such as rice, oil crops, economic crops, medicinal herbs and garden plants to livestocks, including poultry, and freshwater fish. Mineral resources such as coal, natural gas, iron, strontium, limestone, silex and silicon are in great abundance. Its output of oranges and silkworm cocoons ranks first amongst cities in China. It also has a huge potential in harnessing hydraulic power resources.

As the biggest industrial city and economic centre, Chongqing's gross national product (GNP) for 1993 was RMB 33.1 billion with an average increase of 9.8% and it ranked fifth amongst the Chinese cities. Its national income in 1993 was RMB 23.6 billion with an average annual increase of 8.6%. At the turn of the century, Chongqing is expected to achieve an average annual increase of more than 10% in its GNP which means that its GNP will reach RMB 800 billion by the year 2000. In 1995, GNP was over RMB 40 billion. Industrial activities form the main thrusts of Chongqing's economic activities. The total industrial output value reached RMB 44.5 billion in 1993. Currently, there are 8,146 industrial enterprises with more than RMB 20 billion of fixed assets and a labour force of 1.18 million employees. The trades of machinery, metallurgy, chemistry and pharmaceuticals, textile and foodstuff are the key industries in Chongqing, thereby forming a comprehensive industrial system with both heavy and light industries.

As the centre of machinery manufacturing in south-west China and one of the machinery industry bases in China, it produces 81 categories of products with 3,300 specifications and almost 40,000 products. These industries include automobiles, motorcycles, river boats and ships, internal combustion engines, refrigerating machines, storage batteries, me-

---

7 *Business China*, 16 May 1994.

dium and small electrical machinery, water turbo-generators and conventional weapons. In 1992, the total sales from its automobile industry was RMB 8 billion, making Chongqing one of the five national automobile bases in China. Chongqing is one of the nine big steel-making centres and one of the three aluminium fabrication bases in China. It produces more than 120 types of steel products, roll steel products with more than 10,000 specifications, and it manufactures aluminium products with over 13,000 specifications.

Chongqing also plays an important role in the chemical and pharmaceutical industry in south-west China, with a gross industrial output that accounts for about 30% of the total for the region. As a textile industry base in the upper reaches of the Yangtze River, Chongqing has a complete system of textile industry, producing over 2,000 kinds of products of cotton textile, printing, dyeing, silk, wool, ramie, knitting, chemical fibre and textile machinery. The main products of Chongqing's food industry include foodstuff, edible oil, meat products, beverage, cigarettes and canned food. It ranks first in pork, oranges and silkworm cocoon production and second in agricultural output amongst the Chinese cities. Electronic instruments and meters are new industries in Chongqing. Its main electronic products include photoelectric products, telecommunication equipment, optical instrument and computer process controlled equipment.

Chongqing ranks sixth amongst major Chinese cities in its retail sales of goods with a total of 230,000 commercial institutions, markets and facilities. Chongqing is not only the traffic hub for water, land and air transportation but it is also the hub for postal and telecommunication in south-west China. The three trunk railways which provide important transportation links between Chongqing and other major cities of China are the Chengdu-Chongqing, Xiangfan-Chongqing and Sichuan-Guizhou lines. There are also three state highways and eight provincial highways which serve all parts of China. Postal service includes direct mail to over 100 countries all over the world and special express delivery both within and out of China. There are 21 universities and colleges and over 336 scientific and technological research institutions in Chongqing. For the past ten years, Chongqing boasts of more than 6,000 important scientific and technological achievements. Figure 6-2 shows that the distribution of Chongqing's gross output among the industrial and agricultural sector is approximately proportionate to that of Chengdu.

Singapore is an ideal gateway for foreigners intending to invest in Chongqing because Singapore is an established financial centre with good knowledge of the China market. Like its rival city, Chengdu, Chongqing also sent a delegation to Singapore in May 1994, to promote investment opportunities. There are already 32 Singaporean joint ventures in Chongqing. Chongqing also has several promising zones offering preferential investment terms comparable to those in Chengdu, coupled with similar tax holidays for the first two years operation and 50% tax subsidy for the third year in operation. Two important development zones are discussed in the following sections.

FIGURE 6-2
Gross Output of Chongqing

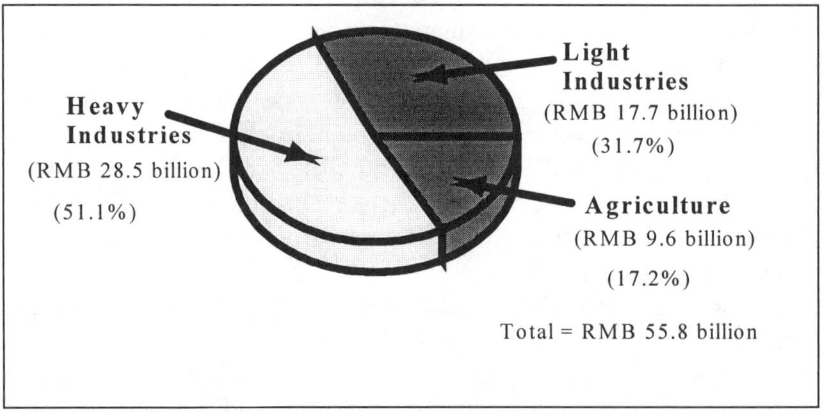

Chongqing Technical Economic Development Zone

The Chongqing Technical Economic Zone was established in August 1990. Over 160 enterprises, including 118 foreign companies with a commitment of US$459 million, have been set up in a zone area of about 100 square kilometres.

Chongqing High and New Technology Industrial Development Zone

The Chongqing High and New Technology industrial development zone contains 600 firms including 30 foreign investment firms. In 1993, the total output of the zone was RMB 467 million which is about US$45 million. By the end of the first quarter of 1994, 132 foreign companies were approved with a total registered capital of US$150 million. The zone consists of two parts, namely, Shapingba, a 225-square kilometre area encompassing the Shazhonglu Scientific and Technical Street and Shiqiaopu Development Zone of High Technology which focuses on electronics and research and development, and the Nanping Industrial Zone of High and New Technology.

SWOT ANALYSIS

Both Chengdu and Chongqing offer a number of advantages and opportunities to potential investors. However, each city also exhibits some disadvantages. The following analysis briefly summarises these factors in terms of each city's strengths, weaknesses, opportunities and threats.

Chengdu

(i) ***Strengths:***

a. Capital of Sichuan province.
b. Personality of local government – encourage and facilitate foreign investment.
c. One-stop management for foreign investors to cut through miles of red tape.
d. Shangli Airport is fourth largest airport in China in terms of cargoes, mails and passengers.
e. Cheaper skilled labour – about 33% lower than open coastal cities.
f. Cheaper land and building materials – prices about one-third of open coastal cities.
g. Rich in agricultural products, mineral and water resources.
h. Able to sell 100% of products to local market.
i. Proximity to large domestic market generated by 110 million consumers in Sichuan.
j. Adequate supply of electricity.
k. Availability of modern telecommunication facilities.

(ii) ***Weaknesses:***

a. Inefficient plants due to ageing, outdated process and over-manning.
b. Ineffective distribution systems – transportation system unable to provide speed and reliability.
c. Airport facilities under renovation.
d. Dependent on rail and road networks for transportation which are currently overburdened and inadequate.
e. Not near to waterways.
f. Difficulty in obtaining local financing for joint ventures.
g. Absence of marketing skills.
h. Difficulty in implementing foreign management concepts in total.
i. Difficulty in valuing Chinese firm – lack of information and absence of market for fixed assets.
j. No clear definition of "high/advanced technology".

(iii) ***Opportunities:***

a. Transformation of existing industries, therefore high priority for foreign investments.
b. Manufacturing that brings in new technology and production methods.
c. Infrastructure developments.
d. Management consultancy and maintenance services.
e. Financial services – Chengdu aims to be financial centre of south-west China.
f. Retail marketing – supermarkets, departmental chains, shopping complexes.
g. Tourist-related industries.
h. Securities-related services – development of security exchange is planned.

(iv) ***Threats:***

a. Competition from Chongqing and other cities.
b. Political risk.

Chongqing

(i) ***Strengths:***

a. Provincial status – autonomous, authority.
b. Industrial and commercial city – Chongqing is the largest in-

dustrial and commercial city in south-west China and has long been a strong scientific and technical centre due to proximity of Chinese military installations. Currently, there are more than 8,000 industrial enterprises with RMB 24.9 billion fixed assets ranking her fifth among China's biggest cities. Industry is Chongqing's main economy. The main industries are machinery, metallurgy, chemicals, pharmaceuticals, textiles and foodstuffs. The city is one of nine big steel-making centres, one of five automobile bases and one of three aluminium fabrication bases in China.

c. Skilled labour – The city has 336 separate research institutes employing 355,000 scientists and technicians.
d. Airport – Modern, all-weather.
e. Personnel of local government.
f. Domestic market – City population of 15 million and provincial population of 110 million.

(ii) ***Weaknesses:***

a. Geographical constraint – mountainous.
b. Traffic congestion – roads are narrow and inadequate.
c. High level of bureaucracy – compartmentalised and cross departmental cooperation is uncommon.
d. Require to maintain positive balance in foreign exchange account.
e. Inadequate telecommunication facilities.

(iii) ***Opportunities:***

a. The manufacture of machine tools has an increasingly important role in China.
b. The attractive zones for investments are: (i) Chongqing Economic and Technical Development Zone (ii) Chongqing High and New Technology Industrial Development Zone.
c. Infrastructure developments.
d. Transformation of existing industries – therefore high priority for foreign investments.
e. Spin off from "Three Gorges Project".

(iv) ***Threats:***

a. Competition from Chengdu and other cities in Sichuan.
b. Political risk.
c. Unfamiliarity with local financial and social systems.

CRITICAL SUCCESS FACTORS

The investment environment in Sichuan varies from place to place. However, several common success factors exist regardless of whether Chengdu or Chongqing is the preferred investment location.

Good Networking (*Guan-xi*)

The importance of *guan-xi* cannot be understated. Throughout our business study mission in Chengdu and Chongqing, we witnessed *guan-xi* as the key factor contributing to success of business ventures.

Right Chinese Partner for Joint Venture

For joint ventures, finding the right partner and getting the relationship right is the crucial factor for success. The Chinese partner who has good connections with the relevant authorities will be able to solve difficult problems and achieve what seems to be impossible. A comprehensive study of joint venture investment in China is presented in research report No. Q204 of the Economic Intelligence Unit entitled "Operating joint ventures in China" by Lois Dougan and Katalin Holzmann.

Third Party Contact

Most Sichuan investment opportunities are made available to companies through a third party. In many joint ventures, disagreements between two parties are often resolved through mediation by the third party.

Good Communication

An investor who is well-versed in the Chinese language and customs will have a competitive edge over other foreign investors in China. Proposals, contracts and other official documents which are written in the Chinese language will avoid the hassles of translation and misinterpretation and will be processed faster. A good interpreter is an alternative to achieve that competitive edge. As investment rules, attitudes and law enforcement vary with the location, good communication is vital in understanding the different local operating conditions.

Thorough Preparation

Successful foreign direct investments are the result of thorough homework and preparation. A good understanding of the Chinese legal, financial and social systems is essential. Investors must be ready to accept the low level of protection accorded to foreign intellectual property and other proprietary rights, including patents and trademarks. Rampant copying of products introduced by foreign investors before an investment is made is not uncommon. In joint ventures, Chinese partners often expect the foreign parties to transfer technology, managerial skills, quality control techniques and worker training.

INVESTMENT OPPORTUNITIES, RISKS AND UNCERTAINTIES

Investment Regulations

Economic reforms, shifting from a centrally planned economy to a market-oriented economy, and years of double-digit growth have begun to transform China's political and social life. Using Gross Domestic Product (GDP) as a measure, China has become Asia's second largest economy. According to the International Monetary Fund's revised GDP measurements, using purchasing power parity rather than exchange rates, China ranks as the world's third largest economy, trailing just behind the economic superpowers – the United States and Japan.

Until recently, most foreign ventures have been set up in the coastal cities where they have enjoyed tax breaks and are closer to export markets. But with parts of the huge Chinese market now opened to foreigners, investors are lured by the massive domestic market of the inner regions and have begun to take a strong interest in the Sichuan province (with a 110 million population) and especially in the two better developed cities of Chengdu and Chongqing. Moreover, foreign investors operating in the special economic and technological development zones of these two cities can receive preferential treatments and enjoy the same privileges that are available in the coastal cities.

Foreign investment in China generally takes one of the following forms:

(i) ***Equity Joint Venture:*** This is a Chinese limited company between a Chinese party and a foreign party established by means of a joint venture contract. The participating parties share profit and risk relative to their respective percentage of equity.

(ii) ***Contractual Joint Venture:*** Unlike an equity joint venture, this form of joint venture does not require a Chinese legal company as a partner. It is established by means of a joint venture contract between the Chinese and foreign parties but the structure allows for considerable flexibility in relation to equity contribution, profit-sharing and assumption of risks.

(iii) ***Wholly Foreign-Owned Enterprise:*** This is a Chinese limited liability company owned entirely by a foreign investor or investors. The scope of activities permitted is generally more restrictive than a joint venture enterprise.

Foreign Investments and Opportunities in Sichuan

One of the key advantages offered by Sichuan to foreign investors is access to the huge domestic market. Sino-foreign ventures in Sichuan are allowed to sell all their wares to the huge domestic market of 110 million consumers. Statistics reported in the China Statistical Yearbook (1993) indicate that Sichuan's GDP and Industrial Output were RMB 149.24 billion and RMB 184.98 billion, respectively. Besides the lucrative domestic market, Sichuan offers lower land costs and cheaper labour compared to the coastal cities. The province also has a large pool of available skilled workers from military factories and other heavy industries.

Preliminary statistics as of February 1994 indicate that there are already more than 4,200 foreign ventures in Sichuan and the countries ranked among the top five in investments are Hong Kong, Taiwan, United States, Singapore and Japan. The foreign ventures in Sichuan vary across a wide spectrum of industries which include infrastructure projects, energy, transportation, construction, property and leisure, electronics and communications, automobiles and motorcycles, electrical machinery and equipment, chemical, precision instruments, textiles, silk, food and beverages, retailing and light and heavy industries.

The opening up of China's huge domestic market presents abundant opportunities. Consumer electronics, household appliances, personal computers and peripherals, telecommunication products (like pagers and mobile phones) are in high demand as Chinese incomes have risen dramatically over the last few years. Similarly, great prospects await foreign ventures in the domestic services market like retail, hotel and tourism.

Investment Risks and Uncertainties

Given the increasing importance of the Chinese domestic market to foreign investors, the surge in foreign investment in China is expected to continue. According to the recent issues of *International Business*, Caterpillar Inc. of the United States is setting up a joint venture to build hydraulic excavators in China with an expected market worth US$2 billion by the year 2000. The Japanese Sanyo Electric Co. has announced a joint venture with a Chinese partner to make 400,000 washing machines annually and NEC Corporation also plans to start producing computers for the Chinese market with a Shanghai partner in the near future. Furthermore, China plans to spend US$41.1 billion in the next six years on telecommunications.

Despite much enthusiasm and the huge potential, doing business in China is not without its problems and some lessons could be learnt from the experience of a joint venture between a state-run company and Hong Kong's Andes Enterprises Ltd. Andes Enterprises, a major distributor of processed seafood, acquired a 60% stake in the Qingdao Canning & Foodstuff Co. and although output of the plant has tripled and productivity is improving sharply, the plant was not breaking even. The reason is that Andes must pay pensions to 700 retired workers which is about as many as the number of its full-time staff. The other issue of dealing with layoffs is just as vexing.

The rush of foreign investment has also given birth to new problems. For example, there are difficulties in finding suitable engineers and managers with a good sense of business. Also, insufficient infrastructure exists. According to a study by Nomura Research Institute as reported in *Asia Business*, China will have to increase its power generation capacity by 20,000 megawatts a year to meet rising demand (the equivalent of building 11 plants the size of the newly opened Daya Bay nuclear power plant in Guangdong) in each of the next six years.

China's political and social situation have thus far been stable although sporadic cases of peasant and student protests have been reported. For the situation to remain under control, it is important that consumer prices be kept under control and the growing gap between rich and poor provinces narrowed. One of the major risks to investors is the devaluation of the Renminbi. Investors should also be aware of increasing corruption. According to a survey by Political Economic Risk Constancy, China ranks high on the list of Asian countries with corrupt business practices. In addition, China's judicial system still proves to be a minefield for many foreign investors. Although many laws have been promulgated, efforts to put these laws into practice are lax.

The Singapore Advantage

The relationship (*guanxi*) between Singapore and China has been superb, and Singapore is well-positioned to be the ideal gateway for foreigners who want to invest in China, especially in Sichuan province. Dr. John Chen, an NTUC assistant secretary-general, has recently been made an adviser to the Chengdu government in China's Sichuan province. He has also been appointed as a provincial adviser to a high-powered steering committee in Sichuan to oversee a S$594 million industrial park project, jointly developed by a Singapore consortium and the city authorities. Dr. Chen will act as a consultant on economic development and widen understanding and economic co-operation between Singapore and the Chinese city. Other Singaporeans who have been made advisers to the Chinese central, provincial or city governments include former cabinet minister Dr. Goh Keng Swee who has been acting as China's economic adviser since 1985, and former chief planner Liu Thai Ker who is an adviser to seven Chinese cities.

In his visit to Singapore in May 1994, Chongqing's mayor Liu Zhizhong encouraged foreign companies which set their eyes on the China market to go through or team up with Singapore because of its good working knowledge of China, the Chinese language and similar cultural backgrounds. As of May 1994, Singapore investments in Chengdu and in Chongqing amounted to US$130 million and US$77 million, respectively.

CONCLUSION

Chengdu and Chongqing are like two sides of a coin, each having its own merits and provide equal chances for successful investments. With increased investments and rapid development in infrastructure in Sichuan province, the two cities will be interconnected by highways, railways and airways in the near future. Transportation between the two cities will be eased and travelling time will be reduced significantly. The high mobility in the factors of production, such as labour and raw materials, between the two cities will render the choice of city for investment to be of less importance.

In deciding on the choice of location, the type of industry, intended market, source of raw materials and the state of local infrastructure are some key factors. Other factors to be considered include productivity, the degree of labour or capital intensity, the supply and ability of labour, and management and administrative flexibility. Living conditions for foreign investors, including traffic conditions, can also influence the choice of location. In a joint venture, the selection of the right partner can dictate the choice of investment sites.

The business environment is dynamic and this affects operating issues. On virtually every operational level, location will make the difference between smooth functioning and a constant battle to get things done. For some investors, being near a market is more crucial than ready access to raw materials; others may prefer the latter and are prepared to ship their products to customers.

The choice of cities, Chengdu or Chongqing, is dependent on the peculiarities of each case.

REFERENCES

Barnathan Joyce, Ergardio Pete, Curry Lynne and Einhorn, Bruce, "China: Birth of a New Economy", *Business Week,* 31 January 1994, pp. 14–20.

Borrus Amy, Barnathan Joyce, Einhorn Bruce and Toy Stewart, "China's Gates Swing Open", *Business Week,* 13 June 1994, pp. 14–15.

"Business Strategies for the PRC", *Business International Asian Research Report,* 1980.

"China wants to join the Club", *The Economist,* 14 May 1994.

Deloitte Touche Tohmatsu (China Office), "Opportunities for Singapore Investment in China", *Economic Bulletin,* September 1993.

"Foreign Investment in the PRC 1991/92", *Jetro China Newsletter,* No. 102, 1993.

"Investing in China – Where, How and Why?", *Economic Intelligence Unit Special Report No. 1071,* January 1987.

Lee Michelle, "MP John Chen named Adviser to Chengdu Government", *The Straits Times,* 16 May 1994.

Linn Gene, "Getting It Right Second Time", *Asia Business,* November 1993, pp. 42–45.

Linn Gene, "The Politics of Power", *Asia Business,* May 1993, p. 9.

Neff Robert, Curry Lynne and Bruce Einhorn, "Asia's Giants Learn to Waltz Together", *Business Week,* 14 March 1994, pp. 20–21.

"Operating Joint Ventures in China", *Economic Intelligence Unit Report No. Q204*, 1993.

"Press Conference on the Investment Environment in China's Chengdu City", *Lianhe Zaobao,* 17 May 1994.

"Sichuan Province – Not So Dark Interior", *Business China,* 16 May 1994.

Statistical Yearbook of Sichuan, China Statistics Press, 1993.

Yu Juan, Kate, "Invest with Singapore, Chinese Mayor urges Foreigners", *The Straits Times,* 4 May 1994.

Zhihua Liu, (Editor-in-Chief), Li Xiangzhu, Jiang Binggao, Qin Xinhua, Gan Jinggang, *Guide to Investment of Chongqing Economic and Technological Development Zone,* Chongqing Municipal Government, 1993.

"Unification of Currency Comes On Stream", *Yazhou Zhoukan*, 16 January 1994.

SECTOR ANALYSIS

Chapter 7

The Choice of Relevant Industries in China*

BY
Alfred BOEY Ghim Cheng
FONG Hin Sing
ZHANG Yan
Peter WOON

INTRODUCTION

NO COUNTRY TODAY is more synonymous with growth, capital gains and vast opportunities to make money than China. Strong economic performances, such as 1993's GDP growth of 12.8%, have been primarily attributed to the flourishing coastal special economic zones (SEZ). However, since 1992, the central government has embarked upon a policy of spreading wealth from the coastal areas to the interior. The inner cities of China are now on the verge of an economic boom. The city of Chongqing, in particular, has been selected to be the "Dragon Head" to spearhead this policy. Potential investors in these regions are now offered a luxury of incentives similar to those offered by the coastal SEZs. These inner cities, typified by the cities of Chengdu and Chongqing, are vastly different in geography, resources and business environments. The

* The authors would like to express their thanks to the project supervisors, Dr. Cao Yong, Associate Professor Chew Soon Beng, Associate Professor J. J. Williams and Dr. Chen Kang for their invaluable advice, guidance and patience.

choice of relevant industries that they are best able to support, and thus provide the investor with the winning competitive edge, is therefore of primary concern.

This chapter provides a brief overview of the investment opportunities available, a classification of the various industrial sectors, and an analysis of the trend of imports and exports in China. This is followed by an analysis of how three particular industries namely, property development, high technology manufacturing and services, are able to fit into the context of the inner cities of Chengdu and Chongqing. Issues pertaining to China's regulations and rules, investors' needs, the inner cities' strengths, capital outlay, investment restrictions and periods of expected return (i.e., long term to short term investment) will be explored. This is a timely analysis in view of the economic boom, the recent relaxations in the types of industries foreigners are allowed to participate in and the potential saturation of good investment opportunities in the coastal SEZs.

INVESTMENT IN CHINA

An Overview of Foreign Investment in China

Initially, the legal environment for foreign investors was not well-defined and little attention was paid to attracting foreign investment. Thus, despite the publicity given to the opening up of China's huge potential market, the amount of foreign investments grew very slowly during the early 1980s due to long and uncertain negotiation processes. This prompted the implementation of a series of regulations in 1983 to better clarify the legal environment for joint ventures. The general problems cited by the early investors were outdated communication and transport systems, serious delivery problems for domestic inputs, archaic labour practices and lack of markets for land — all of which contributed to increasing the cost of doing business in China. Other problems faced were policy induced, and included artificially high valuations of land, labour and other Chinese contributed inputs. The most restrictive of all problems was the requirement to earn foreign exchange which limited access to the billion-person domestic market that had attracted much foreign interest to China. It was only in the later half of the 1980s that serious attention was given to providing incentives for foreign investments. The Provisions for the Encouragement of Foreign Investment was promulgated in October 1986.

Joint ventures received preferential treatment for tax and imports of materials, equipment and vehicles used in production. Explicit encouragement is now given to joint ventures involving advanced technology and the manufacture of exports. Equity joint ventures were granted privileged access to the supply of water, electricity and transportation which meant paying the same price as state-owned enterprises and obtaining interest-free Renminbi (RMB) loans.

In April 1988, the *Law on Co-operative Ventures* was finally passed by the National Peoples' Congress. The legislated investment incentives compared favourably to those offered by other Asian countries. The *Chinese Business Review* (March 1988, pp. 49–51) contains a matrix summarising the investment incentives offered by various Asian countries.

Classifications of Industries

The kinds of industries in China can be grouped under three headings: primary, secondary and tertiary. The primary industries refer to the agricultural and husbandry enterprises. Secondary industries refer to the activities whereby raw resources are processed into products such as the manufacture of steel and machinery. In general, they refer to manufacturing and construction. Tertiary industries refer to the support and service sectors such as retailing, tourism and trucking transportation.

As an indication of the spread of industries in the two cities, 22% of the total outputs from Chongqing is from primary industries, 45% is from secondary industries and 33% is from tertiary industries. Similarly 20% of Chengdu's industrial output comes from primary industries.

In general, the various types of industries can also be broken down by sector classification as shown in Table 7-1.

Import/Export Analysis

The growth in China's foreign trade has been tremendous since the implementation of the open door policy in 1978. Imports have traditionally been greater than exports, thus resulting in a trade deficit that lasted from 1984 to 1989.

The authorities have imposed a licensing system to curb the importation of consumer goods and other non-priority items and also have set up tariffs for certain raw materials needed domestically so as to keep imports under control. Table 7-2 summarises the growth in exports and imports over the ten year period from 1982 to 1992.

TABLE 7-1
Industrial Sector Classifications

Sectors	Descriptions
Building Materials	Building materials and fittings.
Chemicals	Chemicals, plastic materials, gases chemical and petrochemical plant.
Consumer	Consumer goods (not textile).
Electronic	Electronic components, equipment and accessories, electrical equipment, both consumer and industrial.
Engineering	Non-construction-related engineering and services.
Finance	Financing operations.
Food	Food processing, animal foodstuffs and food services.
Machinery	Machinery and machine tools.
Metals	Metal and alloy finished and non-finished products.
Oil	Equipment and services for oil industries.
Packaging	Packaging equipment and materials.
Publishing	Publishing, printing and broadcasting.
Property	Property development, including design, construction and development operating services.
Telecoms	Telecommunications equipment.
Textile	Textile plants, garment manufacturing and related items.
Transport	Transportation (vehicles and services), shipping and related items.
Misc.	Miscellaneous.

Source: Extracted from *A Strategic Guide to EJV in China*, Nigel Campbell, 1989.

TABLE 7-2
Value and Percent of GDP

Sectors	Year	Value	Percentage
Exports	1982	\$21.9b	7.9%
	1992	\$85b	19.6%
Imports	1982	\$18.9b	6.8%
	1992	\$80.6b	18.6%

Analysis of Exports

One of the main goals of China's trade policy is to increase the percentage share of manufactured goods in the country's total exports. There is an increasing trend towards more sophisticated manufactured items, including machinery and transport equipment, as a result of high foreign investment in these sectors. In 1992, the export share of these items rose by about 86% as compared to the same period in the previous year. Textile and footware accounted for one-third of 1992's exports or US$28 billion. High foreign investment in capital-intensive areas have also spawned an increase in exports of machinery, electronic products and transport equipment. China's main trading partners are the U.S., the European Community, Japan and Hong Kong. Hong Kong is the top destination for Chinese exports. She is a major re-export centre for Chinese goods, most of which are transhipped to industrialised markets.

Analysis of Imports

To satisfy the demands of the domestic needs and also to meet the goals of modernisation, China's imports have continued to expand and diversify. The Sino-U.S. agreement signed in October 1992 on opening China's market has led to more imports in 1993, 1994 and 1995. Based on the agreement, China eliminated 75% of her import restrictions by the end of 1995 and will lift the remaining controls by the end of 1997. Machinery and transport equipment are the largest import category while chemicals, manufactured goods, steel, textile yarn and fertiliser constitute the rest of the imports.

PROPERTY DEVELOPMENT SECTOR

Property Development in China

By the end of 1992, the total number of property developers in China had risen to a total of 12,400. Investors, first from Hong Kong and then from other parts of South-east Asia, rushed to develop commercial, industrial and residential property in China. This created a boom in the real estate market which was already absorbing hundreds of millions of local currency. As a result, the property investment for the year 1992 was reported to be RMB 33.2 billion, an increase of 124% as compared to 1991. In addition, a total area of 23,340 acres of land was used for property development. This accounts for the increase of 175% of the total amount of land area used.

For various reasons, many overseas Chinese have obtained land development rights in China. There are also traders and manufacturers who originally bought land to cope with the expansion of their business operations. Although the country is now more open to economic development, many investors have taken the opportunity to lunge into the property market, confident that the country's 1.2 billion population will provide the demand to support their investments. In addition, with the economy prospering, there is a growing demand for high quality office space, especially in the southern part of the country where multinational companies are located. Basically, for an industry which includes property development and real estate investment it would be more suited for short to medium-term returns.

The boom in property development is also fuelled by speculative fever, particularly among Hong Kong investors and China's small, but growing, entrepreneurial class. Rampant speculation has pushed prices in some areas to unrealistic levels. Property prices in the southern part of the country, especially in places like Guangdong and Shenzhen, have undergone the steepest increment because of hazardous speculation. Shenzhen's property prices for instance, have outdone the boom in Hong Kong, shooting up almost 80% compared with an average of 60% in Hong Kong. It has reached a stage where there is no way a local person can afford the current market prices. In Shanghai and Beijing, however, speculation is less intense. Officials in these two areas are making efforts to further simulate the property market.

In the inner states of China such as Sichuan province, the property market industry is a lucrative and favourable industry. This is further complemented by the abundance of undeveloped land, cheap labour cost, availability of raw materials, keen interests of foreign investors and strong economic growth in these areas.

Property projects in China are normally infrastructure-driven. The price of a land site often includes the need to build roads, reservoirs and railways for the local government. Usually, the developer identifies a site for investment and the authorities add a list of infrastructure requirements as a condition of ownership. The land price is discounted to take into account infrastructure developments and property development as a means of funding the facility and generating a reasonable return simultaneously.

Property Development in Sichuan

The property development or real estate industry within Sichuan constitutes about 22% of all the industries. The manufacturing industry, at 69%, had the largest percentage of the total industries in the province. Although there has been a reduction in real estate investments in recent months, the perception is that property development is still a potential investment opportunity for foreigners. Basically, property development can be categorised under three main types, namely:

(a) industrial sites;
(b) commercial sites; and
(c) residential and villa sites.

The lease for the land-use rights for industrial sites ranges from 50 to 55 years, commercial sites from 40 to 45 years, and for residential and villa sites the lease period is 70 years. The average prices for the various sites in Sichuan are as follows: industrial sites are priced at RMB 276 per square metre; commercial sites are priced at RMB 736 per square metre; residential sites are priced at RMB 368 per square metre and villa sites are priced at RMB 600 per square metre.

In terms of the investment in property development in Sichuan, Chengdu and Chongqing account for about 65% of the total amount invested. With property development in China skewed towards the coastal areas such as Beijing, Shanghai, and border areas like Guangdong and Shenzhen, the inner states offer the best opportunities for investment. Investment in this industry is suited for short to medium term.

Although foreigners can buy properties in China, the real estate projects are targeted mainly at the domestic market. In fact, it was mentioned by one of the delegates from Chongqing that the property market in China as a whole is mainly aimed at the primary market, that is, the buyers intend to occupy the property that they have bought. The secondary market, such as resale and rental, has not been as profitable as one might have thought. The returns are meagre compared with that of other developing countries such as Singapore. In fact, it was reported that the rental for lodgings provided by the government for the local people ranged from a mere RMB 150 to RMB 200 per month for an average three-room apartment. This policy has adversely affected the property rental market.

During the boom in property development in 1992, there was a lack of control on the type of property that the developer could build. This has resulted in a propensity to develop more profitable properties such as commercial and industrial sites. In addition, the lack of efficient laws and regulations to control the property market has led to frantic speculation from both local and foreign investors. However, as of 1 January 1994, speculation has been diminished somewhat with the promulgation of the new taxation system. In Sichuan, the sale of a property incurs a 5% sales tax. In addition, 33% of capital gains will be taxed, 30% representing payment for government tax and 3% for provincial tax.

According to Professor Yang Kang from the Institute of Economic Reform, Sichuan Academy of Social Sciences, the purchasing power of the people in Sichuan was estimated to be about 70% of that of their counterparts in coastal cities like Shanghai. However, based on their income of RMB 3,000 to RMB 6,000 per annum and the market price of the residential apartments and villas, it is apparent that they would not be able to afford the properties. Furthermore, the market for rental and resale of apartments is almost non-existent because the government provides cheap housing for its citizens.

Although the price of properties in Sichuan is not within the reach of the majority of citizens, properties situated within the prime areas are in high demand. The types of property buyers can be categorised into three basic profiles:

(a) local Chinese who have amassed fortunes overseas and who have returned to China to invest in property;
(b) successful local businessman investing in commercial, industrial and residential property in China; and
(c) foreigners who have bought property for their relatives who reside in mainland China.

Technical Analysis

The climate for property development in Sichuan province is conducive for investment regardless of whether the enterprise is a joint venture or wholly owned. Taking into consideration various factors such as the availability of raw materials and natural resources, and the abundance of undeveloped land, investment in this industry is strongly encouraged. Other factors such as the low production cost, strong economic growth, large domestic market, state of the art technology, and foreign investment interests in south-west China, have added to the potential of the property industry in Sichuan.

In fact, according to a speaker from the Chongqing municipal government, building and raw materials in Sichuan are about three times cheaper compared to the coastal areas. Correspondingly, wages and salary of workers within the inner states are about three times less than those in the coastal areas. The cheap labour cost, of RMB 3,000 – RMB 6,000 per annum, the huge potential, and the availability of skilled labour, has made property investment very attractive.

In Chongqing, the municipal government township has earmarked two economic and technological development zones namely, the Nan Ping and Jiang Bei, to be developed into a technological and a residential zone respectively. On the other hand, in Chengdu, Jiu Liu Ba has been designated for development into a residential zone. Therefore, property developers have diverse investment options. In these development zones, preferential treatment and guidance is rendered by management. The management staff of these zones also provides assistance in processing applications for governmental approval and in the search for a suitable local partner. This reduces voluminous paperwork. For instance, the Brilliant Company in Chengdu's economic and developmental zone is responsible for managing and helping foreign investors set up business in Chengdu.

One of the main disadvantages of the inner states, as compared to the coastal and border states, is the transportation system. Chengdu, the capital of Sichuan, presently has three railway tracks linking it to Chongqing, Bao Ji and Kun Ming with another track linking it to Da Xian in the planning stage. At the end of 1994, the highway between Chongqing and Chengdu was completed. With the improved transport system, raw materials, supplies, products, and other resources will be more readily available. Building materials and state-of-the-art designs and technologies can be easily imported making property development opportunities in Sichuan more promising.

Financial/Economic Analysis

The expected rate of return for a typical property development in Chongqing was reported to be 33% within the first three years. It is expected to be a highly profitable industry especially when more land is released by the government for property development. One example of a successful property developer in Sichuan is Wearnes Brothers which has invested in residential properties in Chengdu and Chongqing. Both the Orchard Villa in Chengdu and the Orchard Manor in Chongqing are property developments located in the economic development zones. Both of these developments are joint ventures, with Wearnes Brothers holding 95% of the total shares of the enterprise.

According to one local manager, Orchard Manor in Chongqing has seen good returns within nine months of launching Phase One of the entire project. Out of a total of 40 villas and 24 units of private apartments, 15 were snapped up within months of the launch. The cost of each villa was priced at RMB 1.5 million, or approximately S$275,000 per unit.

Prospects

Property development will become an important industry. Revenue from property development in developed countries is estimated to be about 20% of GDP. Currently, revenue derived from property development in China is only about 2.7%, indicating the huge potential for this industry.

The rate of return on property is high. According to one newspaper article, whilst most industries may earn a rate of return ranging from 10 to 12%, property development earns rates varying from 20 to 30%. In fact, in some areas like Shenzhen and Guangdong, the rate of return is approximately 50%. Because of the high rates of return, many foreign investors have invaded the Chinese market particularly through foreign-local joint ventures and wholly owned foreign investments.

The demand for residential property is expected to be high. By the end of 1992, the average occupied area per person was 7.3 square metres. To arrive at the target of 8 square metres per person set by the government, China must construct an additional 150 to 180 million residential buildings.

Comments

While the returns from property investment in China can be very good, there are risks for the unwary investor not accustomed to an uncertain market with a poor legal framework. China is in the process of opening its door to the outside world and policies that have been promulgated can be subject to change. The investor should tread carefully in this market.

MANUFACTURING

In 1992, manufacturing projects in China amounted to US$32.7 billion or 56% of total direct investments. Traditionally, manufacturing has been confined to highly labour-intensive products such as textiles and consumer electronics, which were targeted mainly for export. This business strategy of producing for export is appropriate because it uses China's huge and inexpensive workforce without violating her regulations on foreign cash flows and the restrictions to sell directly to the local market. In the two years since 1992, some of these restrictions have been relaxed in order to encourage high technology manufacturing, for instance allowing up to 100% of high technology foreign venture products to be sold domestically and granting permission for multinationals to balance foreign currency flows among their companies. This relaxation of restrictions has met with some success as several major MNCs, such as Philips and IBM, have secured rights to set up branch operations. Strategically, it also allows long-term penetration of the domestic market. Sichuan province itself has a potential consumer market of 110 million people. According to the Hong Kong based market research group Concord, there were 80 million people in China in 1992 with incomes of at least US$7,500 per annum. With subsidised housing and relatively cheap cost of living, this translates into consumers with substantial savings and buying power.

The definition of "hi-tech" is subjective. However, from visits to the development parks and joint venture companies, it was ascertained that hi-tech referred to new technology (either manufacturing processes or products) not currently or widely available in China. As an example, the Jialing-Yamaha joint venture which produces motorcycles comes under this category although the equipment and product models have been available in Japan for some time. Another example of a hi-tech concern is the Taiwanese joint venture of Trusnex Food Co. Ltd. in Chengdu. It was formed using Chinese food technology and Taiwanese manufacturing technology, management and finance. In the inner cities, such as Chengdu and Chongqing, hi-tech manufacturing processes primarily targeted at the domestic market is a viable option.

The State Planning Commission in 1993 announced policies encouraging projects using new technologies. In Chengdu, preferential investments terms are available in the technology parks. Examples are the Chengdu High and New Technology Development Zone, Chengdu-Singapore Industrial Garden and the Longquan Development Zone. Similarly, in Chongqing, its Technical Economic Development Zone and its High and New Technology Industrial Development Zone have attracted investments. Some of the preferential investment terms include tax exemptions for the first two years followed by a reduced rate of 10 to 15% for the subsequent three years.

Infrastructure

As in any manufacturing environment, hi-tech manufacturing needs good supporting infrastructure in terms of power, water, telecommunications and transportation networks. Poor supporting facilities will ultimately lead to high operating costs and unnecessary losses. Of major concern to the investor is the ability of the inner cities to provide such facilities efficiently. Present facilities in the technological parks are not all up to par. Power outages and lack of IDD lines, especially in Chengdu, are of primary concern. However, the situation is improving and the central government has been reported to have set aside RMB 500 million to improve the infrastructure. In terms of power and water, there is already an infrastructure to provide these facilities and it is expected to be improved further with the completion of the three gorges dam. In terms of transportation, the inner cities lack in comparison with the coastal cities. However, with the completion and operation of new rail extensions in 1995 and the proposed RMB 1.13 billion investment in highways to form a land-and-water coordinated transport network, transportation is expected to improve within the Sichuan region. The current situation as reported by the general manager of the Chengdu Brilliant Development Co. Ltd. suggests a period of 4–7 days for goods to be transported to the coastal cities.

Chongqing has the added advantage of being accessible by ship from Wuhan and Shanghai. This city could play an important role in the future by serving the hinterland of Sichuan. It is, however, similarly plagued with transportation problems. Traffic jams within the city itself are not uncommon. Again, the transport situation is expected to improve with the completion of several road projects and highway construction which are currently in progress. In the short term, this lack of a good infrastructure will affect the start up cost and initial operating efficiency. However, the commitment of the municipal and central governments, and the ensuing pace of infrastructure development currently going on, are encouraging signs of better things to come.

Supporting Industries

Of primary concern to hi-tech manufacturing is the availability of supporting industries. In the case of electronics manufacturing, supporting industries such as PCBAs manufacturing are a necessity. The alternatives of importing these sub-products or manufacturing are not always the most efficient strategy. Extensive imports as inputs for manufacturing would, however, imply increased operating cost and the subsequent erosion of any competitive advantage gained from the availability of inexpensive labour.

Examining the existing local enterprises in and around the two cities suggests that the region is still primarily based on heavy industries such as mining, chemical processing, steel making and machinery manufacturing. This is well-suited for hi-tech manufacturing industries related to products such as automobiles and heavy machinery. The current situation of lack of support industries that are in themselves hi-tech (e.g., PCBAs manufacturing) can be a dilemma as well as an opportunity. There exists an opportunity for such contract manufacturers of sub-products to penetrate the region together with their MNC customers.

This problem of support industries is not insurmountable for certain OEM products. In the case of the Puyi-Briggs Stratton joint venture which produces outboard motors, it has been able to co-operate with local industries to source more than 40 subparts for its production.

An additional consideration is supporting services such as staff functions (e.g., book-keeping and accounting). Employing such services may be difficult and the ideal solution therefore may be to locate a local partner with such resources already at hand.

Resources

The Sichuan basin has many raw mineral and resources such as coal and iron. This provides for inexpensive manufacturing inputs for the heavy industries. These are of lesser importance, however, for hi-tech manufacturing where there is a greater need for sub-products that are already semi-processed as in precision machined parts and PCBA parts.

Workforce

The level of skills required of an operator in hi-tech manufacturing is usually above average. Some level of expertise (either academic or technical) will be needed either for more complex assembly work or operating of machines. Based on feedback from the visit to the Puyi-Briggs Stratton factory, substantial training was needed for the work-force to adapt to international standards. This is especially important if the final goods produced are meant not only for the local market but for international sales where international quality standards must be adhered to.

There are abundant universities and research institutes located in Sichuan which can supply a good technical workforce. The city of Chongqing is reported to have some 336 separate research institutes employing 335,000 scientists and technicians. This provides a ready pool of talent that can be utilised.

Wages on average in Chengdu and Chongqing range from RMB 300 to RMB 600 a month. This compares favourably with the average monthly wage of RMB 800 in cities such as Guangdong.

Manufacturing often involves complicated process instructions. The medium of instruction (written or spoken) is often in a foreign language. Competent translation of these process instructions will be required. This was cited as of prime importance by the spokesman from the Jialing-Yamaha factory.

Markets

The inner cities of Chengdu and Chongqing are major cities with populations of 9 and 15 million, respectively. In addition, these cities are gateways serving the Sichuan basin which has a total of 110 million people. This potentially lucrative internal market is basically still in its infancy. With the careful selection of the right local joint venture partner, marketing and distribution to these areas can be established quickly.

Prospects

The prospect of hi-tech manufacturing in products such as cars and machinery is good. These products basically fit well into the urban environment in terms of the large number of support industries, the low cost of labour and the large untapped domestic market, and they are not greatly affected by the deficiencies in urban transportation. In addition, these industries are encouraged by the municipal government and, in a country where relationship or *guanxi* still plays a major role, this could mean a much smoother start up and eventual operation.

SERVICE SECTOR

The service sector encompasses a wide and diversified set of investment opportunities. There are three areas in the service sector that have very good prospects and growth potential. The three areas are:

(i) the advertising industry;
(ii) management consultancy services; and
(iii) financial services.

Opportunities in Advertising Industry

Fuelled by a consumer boom and a growing demand for imported luxuries by Chinese consumers, the advertising industry is currently becoming one of the highest revenue generating industries. In 1991, spending on advertising, including billings and production, rose 40.26% to US$636.8 million. Guangdong is first, and it accounted for one-fifth of this amount which is a 60% rise over 1990 and triple the 1988 total of RMB 210 million.

All across China, propaganda and political news which used to

increase since the beginning of 1993.

The types of foreign institutions in China include foreign-funded banks, Sino-foreign co-funded banks, co-funded financial companies, branches of foreign banks, branches of foreign insurance companies and other forms. They collect around 8% of bank deposits from foreign countries but mainly offer loans in China.

In the first half of 1992, the number of foreign funded projects reached 10,000 and involved negotiated foreign capital of US$58.76 billion with US$9.40 billion actually put into use. Foreign banks enjoy preferential policies. For example, Shanghai stipulates that foreign financial institutions can be exempt from income tax for the first profit-making year. Their rate is only 7.5% in the second and third year and in the following years their rate is set at 15%. Domestic banks (state-owned), on the other hand, are levied at the rate of 55%. In the past two years, amidst new waves of opening to the outside world, some provinces and cities have been setting up financial and trade areas and have worked out their own preferential measures to attract foreign financial institutions.

Practice over the past decade shows that foreign banks can enjoy profits in China. Take the Shenzhen Special Economic Zone for example. From 1982 to the end of 1992, 16 branches of foreign banks, an insurance sub-company, a Sino-foreign co-funded financial company and ten representative offices of foreign banks have been set up there. Most of the banks suffered losses in the first year, maintained a balance between income and expenditure in the second year and obtained profits in the third year. Foreign exchange volume provided by foreign banks in Shenzhen constitutes 4% of the city's total foreign currency. Guangdong's floating glass factory, Shenzhen Evergreen Flower Co. and other projects all have obtained loans from foreign banks in Shenzhen to aid their construction.

Shanghai's foreign banks and financial companies have become more crucial to the city's financial system. Statistics show that the total asset value of foreign banks and co-funded financial institutions in Shanghai reached US$58 million in 1992. Out of this, forex loans increased 127% over 1991 and the balance of foreign currency deposits rose 134.3%. The balance of export accounts in the Shanghai area reached US$811 million which is 25% of the city's total business volume in this field. Moreover, foreign banks have also taken an active part in extending loans organised by banks. Loans already provided and under negotiation total over US$100 million.

In addition to the continuous growth of their assets, various financial institutions have made dramatic progress in business services. Some have been chosen as clearing banks for Shanghai's B shares. Many branches of foreign banks have also directly introduced foreign enterprises to invest in Shanghai. Concerned financial administrative departments in Shanghai have not only provided active support to foreign banks to develop their business in areas such as foreign currency deposits, loans and international settlement, but they have also helped them to open limited Renminbi business.

The Bank of Netherlands, ABN-AMRO, which has assets of 250 billion, started business in China in the early 1980s. Now it covers services such as projects, joint ventures, syndicated loans, export credit and international trade. Apart from actively participating in syndicated loans in Shanghai, the bank also undertakes the sale of several kinds of B shares abroad.

The largest foreign bank in China, the Hong Kong and Shanghai Banking Corp., has set up branches in Shanghai, Shenzhen, Xiamen and Qingdao. In 1989, it was approved as a broker of the Shanghai Foreign Currency Exchange Centre. In June 1991, with the support of Asian Development Bank, it organised a group of banks to finance the construction of Nan-pu Bridge.

Admittedly, China's current financial system does not compare favourably with international financial structures. For example, service trades are undeveloped, funds lack fluidity and financial markets are imperfect. There is no access to information on new products between the Chinese and foreign banks. The majority of Chinese in the field are unacquainted with globally common bank operation technologies. Therefore, China requires many laws and regulations such as those that cover banks, contracts, companies and stocks.

The Chinese government is making efforts to improve its financial environment and strengthen the legal structure. In September 1988, the Shanghai Foreign Currency Exchange Centre was founded which was the first open body of its kind in China. By 1991, the centre's annual transaction volume reached US$2.4 billion. On 1 June 1992, it added futures trading of foreign exchange. In November 1990, China's first stock exchange was set up in Shanghai followed by a stock exchange in Shenzhen.

The government has recently set up the China Trust and Investment Corporation for Economic Development (CTICED) to tap international funds for mega projects in the country. For a start, the CTICED has successfully raised US$20 million in its maiden syndication in Singapore on 28 April 1993. CTICED's three-year loan was arranged by the Singapore branch of Monte dei Pashi di Siena.

CONCLUSION

In conclusion, the environment for investment opportunities is very favourable and China as a whole has recognised the significance of foreign investment in its move towards modernisation. This has prompted the Chinese leaders and authorities to implement economic reforms, policies and regulations to promote and encourage foreign investment. The authorities have also drafted a list of priority areas for investment which includes property development, hi-tech manufacturing, and service industries.

REFERENCES

Campbell Nigel, *A Strategic Guide to Equity Joint Ventures in China,* Pergamon Press, New York, 1989.

China's Foreign Policy, New Star Publishers, 1993.

Foreign Banks in China, New Star Publishers, 1993.

Pomfret Richard, *Investing in China — Ten Years of the "Open Door" Policy,* Harvester Wheatsheaf, 1991.

Tan Cheng Leong and Terence T. S. Lim, *China — Business and Investment Opportunities*, Cassia Business Intelligence Series, 1993.

Chapter 8

The Electronics Sector in China

BY
CHOW Poh Heng

INTRODUCTION

THE PEOPLE'S REPUBLIC of China (PRC) has become the focus of much attention in recent years. Despite global capital constraint and anaemic growth in world trade, China has achieved remarkable rates of economic growth. In 1993, China's economy grew by 13%. That expansion spilled over into 1994 and the economy grew at 11.6% in GDP terms.

Singapore was the sixth largest investor in China in 1993, and trade in electronics with China rose 74% to S$422 million in 1993 over the previous year. Against this background, this chapter attempts to:

(i) Evaluate the various aspects of China's electronics sector potential;
(ii) Pinpoint foreseeable risks and investment regulations in China; and
(iii) Analyse the impact on Singapore's electronics industry caused by the relocation of local electronics production lines to China.

CHINA'S ELECTRONICS INDUSTRY

This section will provide an analysis of the various aspects of China's electronics sector potential. Before proceeding further, a few preliminary comments on terminology are in order. The electronics industry covers a vast array of activities commonly divided into three categories: (1) consumer electronics; (2) component electronics; (3) industrial electronics. These categories and their related activities are shown in Table 8-1.

TABLE 8-1
Components of the Electronics Industry

Consumer Electronics	Component Electronics	Industrial Electronics
Colour TV	Semiconductors	Disk drives
Radio cassette	Colour picture tubes	Computer system
TV receivers subassemblies	Capacitors	Telecommunication equipment
Car radio/tape player	Resistors	Printer
Video cassette recorder	Condenser	Terminal
Others	Others	Tape drives
		Others

The electronics industry has assumed a dominant place in the Chinese economy. According to the Ministry of Machinery and Electronics, the industry accounted for a significant portion of manufacturing investment and the total output value for more than 8,900 electronics enterprises nationwide stood at RMB 105 billion or 5% of manufacturing output in 1992. It is in this context that the Chinese government has designated the electronics sector as one of the growth industries in its development strategy for the 1990s.

The identification of the electronics sector as a vital industry by the Chinese government is an emulation of the development paths of the successful Newly Industrialising Economies (NIEs) which invested heavily in the production of electronics outputs both for domestic market and export.

China's electronics industry is mainly concentrated in the coastal regions – Shanghai, Jiangsu, Guangdong, Tianyian and Beijing. The only non-coastal province with a sizeable electronics industry is Sichuan.

Consumer Electronics

Flourishing sales of consumer electronics in China have reached their peak in recent years and traditional consumer electronics are expected to level off. According to the Ministry of Machinery and Electronics, the 1993 output value for electronics products in the consumption category was RMB 58.8 billion in 1993 and was over RMB 70 billion in 1994, a 19% increase over the previous year. Demand for high-end consumer electronics like air conditioners, personal computers and telephones is likely to emerge as a new focus of consumption.

In terms of world demand for consumer electronics, growth in this sector is expected to be slow as most of the products (TV, VCRs, Camcorders) in the major markets of the OECD countries have matured. Major multinationals such as Matsushita, Sony and Sanyo which dominate this sector, have either seen their profits dropping substantially or are even experiencing losses (Sanyo).

Substantial growth in this sector can be expected only if new products take off in a big way like the "Walkman" or camcorders. HDTV has been introduced by the Japanese but the EEC and U.S.A. have not accepted it yet as they are trying to develop their own versions. Digital compact cassettes and minidisc players have been launched but it is too early to gauge consumer response to these two new consumer electronics products. Notwithstanding the many favourable conditions in the consumer electronics sector like short development and production cycles, high value-added and short term recovery of capital, the industry is experiencing lacklustre demand and caution must be exercised when considering investment in this sector that is targeted at the world market.

Component Electronics

The output value for the component electronics category in China for 1993 was RMB 43.2 billion and the Ministry of Machinery and Electronics reported an increase of more than 18% in 1994 to over RMB 51 billion. Within this subsector, semiconductors are used in many applications in the industrial and consumer markets. They are capable of storing data and are tiny circuits on a chip which form the heart of modern computers. Being intelligent in that sense, and because of its tiny size and relatively inexpensive costs, semiconductors can be used to make products which are highly accurate, reliable and intelligent.

The demand for semiconductor devices varies between products and end-users. Integrated circuits (ICs) comprise the bulk of the consumption of products shipped by the semiconductor industry. The computer industry remains the major end-user sector, followed by office equipment, telecommunication, consumer and industrial electronics.

Semiconductors and integrated circuits are currently in short supply in China and a large portion must be imported from abroad. This is due to the past when Chinese manufacturers of component electronics were state-owned enterprises involved in low quality, high cost production. Prices for their products are most often 40 to 50% higher than those from overseas. In recent years, however, dozens of enterprises have established joint ventures with foreign companies to produce high quality products at low cost. As a result, state-owned enterprises have been faced with a difficult situation.

The world's semiconductors industry took a downturn after showing some recovery in the 1988–90 period due to the slowing down in the economies of the industrialised countries. The semiconductor industry was badly hit by lack of orders from its biggest customer — the computer industry. However, the market has recovered somewhat and it is currently buoyed by a healthy demand for PCs and telecommunication electronics such as cellular phones. Worldwide demand for semiconductors is expected to continue to grow and many industrial analysts have touted semiconductors as the "oil of the 21st century".

Industrial Electronics

Market demand for industrial electronics is thriving and continues to increase at a rapid rate. In terms of output value, electronics products in the industrial category reached more than RMB 3.9 billion yuan in 1994, a rise of over 30%.

A number of industrial electronics products that are in high demand include equipment for satellite communications stations, mobile communications equipment, programmed control television exchanges, mini-computers, computer hardware and software. The demand for such products is expected to remain high in the near term.

It has been widely reported in the media that major players in the industrial electronics subsector such as IBM, Digital Equipment and Olivetti are "deconstructing" — closing factories, cutting jobs, spinning off subsidiaries and slashing staff size. Companies like Apple and Compaq have laid off thousands to cut down overhead costs in order to keep their market share.

With the big players in electronics slashing their manufacturing operations and outsourcing components and services, one sector of the industry that is reaping the rewards is contract manufacturing. Being one of the relatively low cost manufacturing countries for electronics components, China should be able to secure some of the original equipment manufacturing (OEM) business of the world's major computer makers which are seeking relatively lower cost manufacturing sites and sources in the developing Asian nations.

Against the background mentioned above, the inflow of foreign investment in the component and industrial electronics subsectors is expected to be strong. The support is expected to come from the improving worldwide sales of PCs and telecommunication equipment which would spur higher demand for semiconductors and other industrial electronics component.

RISKS AND INVESTMENT REGULATIONS

Notwithstanding the risks of continued depreciation of the Renminbi and the overheating of the economy, one of the main concerns to Singapore's manufacturing establishments is that infrastructural development in China has significantly lagged behind the country's economic progress. In particular, the overloading of the domestic transport system has raised serious concern. In 1992, rail freight, which accounted for the bulk of distribution across the country, rose by a mere 3%. This compares to a 20.8% growth in industrial production in the same year. Although the government is committed to invest some RMB 120 billion over the next four years to upgrade the country's infrastructure network, investors must be cautious when planning their manufacturing bases, distribution channels and/or retail outlets so as to minimise any possible losses due to transportation delay.

On the other hand, the electronics industry is likely to benefit from China's proposed deep tax cuts in the network of industrial parks. China is establishing a country-wide network of industrial parks with a view to attract foreign and domestic investments in high technological enterprises. Since 1991, the government has approved the legal framework for 27 high-tech industrial parks. These parks are expected to play a significant role in bridging the technological gap in the electronics industry. In addition, foreign joint-ventures are completely exempted from income taxes for the first two profit-making years. The income tax rate for joint ventures is 33% but high-tech ventures in industrial parks are subject to a tax rate of 15%. The tax rate will be reduced to 10% for companies exporting over 70% of their total production.

THE IMPACT ON SINGAPORE'S ELECTRONICS INDUSTRY CAUSED BY THE RELOCATION OF PRODUCTION LINES TO CHINA

The electronics industry has played a dominant role in the Singapore economy accounting for 40.8% of manufacturing output and 40% of domestic exports in 1993. To understand how Singapore can actually benefit from the moving of electronics production lines to countries like China, we must have an overview of the electronics sector in Singapore, the market that it serves, and the revolution in global electronics and telecommunications.

Singapore's electronics production is centred on multinational groups which were lured to set up manufacturing facilities in the 1970s. To support this growth, a wide range of supporting industries mushroomed, especially as local engineers gained experience with firms like Hewlett Packard, IBM, Apple and Matsushita. Apart from production, Singapore is increasingly important as a sourcing, design, engineering and research centre for major players in the electronics industry.

The accumulation of managerial, engineering, programming, design and R&D skills over 20 years gives Singapore a major advantage for the location of leading-edge production facilities. As more and more of the brainwork is being done here, it becomes increasingly difficult for MNCs to contemplate wholesale relocation from Singapore, though lower-grade manufacturing is filtering down to other countries in the region.

Due to acute labour shortages, many of the smaller local electronics subcontractors are facing tough times as the MNCs are moving their most intensive production lines to Batam, Johor and Penang. Cheap labour in China is also attracting some producers. For example, Texas giant, Compaq, has announced plans to set up a new plant assembling printed circuit board in China – the kind of work it has previously given to local subcontractors in Singapore. IPC also has plans for new factories in China to make notebook computers and multimedia which so far have been subcontracted to Singapore firms.

Disk drives manufactured in Singapore (50% of the domestic electronics output) accounted for over half of the world's production in 1993. This ratio is expected to fall over time. Older generation machines are now being made in Penang, Thailand, and lately, in China. Conner Peripherals, for example, launched production in Singapore and, as the product matured, shifted production to Penang and Shenzhen to reduce costs. Relocation helped contain assembly costs, but engineering and component manufacturing are less likely to be sited elsewhere as they cannot be easily moved.

One thing these firms share in common is that they are leaders in their respective market segments and they appear ready to move in this direction because of economies of scale. They no longer need to "share" their profit margins with subcontractors and shift their less lucrative, low-margin and labour-intensive jobs towards Malaysia, Batam, Thailand and China.

Such regional relocation, far from weakening Singapore's position, will actually entrench its importance to electronics companies. For a number of low grade local electronics companies, there is a tendency that these low-value operations will be blown away in the first storm should the electronics industry experience a downturn. We take the view that there is little Singapore can do to hold their labour-intensive assembly operations. The relocation of labour-intensive manufacturing plants to lower cost countries suggests that higher-technology businesses will still find Singapore an ideal regional base.

Singapore has much to gain from establishing China-based manufacturing facilities designed for export based on the following reasons.

Inexpensive Land and Labour

China has ample inexpensive land and labour despite the huge inflows of foreign capital in recent years which have been driving up wages and the prices of leasehold land. The average annual wages of RMB 3,468 in China are still low compared with workers' wages in Singapore of RMB 74,613 in 1993.

Depreciation of Renminbi

In January 1994, the steep depreciation of the Chinese Renminbi (RMB) has made investing in China even cheaper by 50%. Economists still believe that the RMB will continue losing value to the U.S. dollar by another 15% in the long term as China's membership of the General Agreement on Tariffs and Trade (GATT) requires a free-floating currency approach.

Language, Politics and Culture

The relationship between Singapore and China is arguably stronger than for any other country in the world. Because Mandarin is an official language of both countries, Singapore businessmen find it easier to communicate throughout China than their Hong Kong counterparts who are predominantly Cantonese-speaking.

Although the Taiwanese can speak both Mandarin and local dialects, the governments of Taiwan and Beijing do not officially recognise each other. As long as political frictions exist, Singapore investors will receive a greater degree of co-operation and support from China's provincial government than Taiwan would.

Moreover, China's provincial governments are uncomfortable about dealing with large, foreign MNCs. They prefer smaller projects which allow them greater control over events. China's infamous bureaucracy also tends to interfere more heavily with large projects. As a result, Singapore firms may find it easier to get started in an environment which is still suspicious of the intentions of large foreign MNCs.

CONCLUSION

In view of the present situation and future outlook of China's electronics industry, the following recommendations can be made.

(i) Investing in the semiconductors segment can still be considered although it is important that the manufacturer has the technical expertise and financial resources to keep abreast of the latest technology as this segment is characterised by short product cycles, high R&D and investment costs, and generally low margins.

(ii) The personal computers and telecommunication equipment segments have good growth potential and provide some scope for investment. However, it is again important that a manufacturer is able to respond quickly to rapidly changing market requirements, to be cost-competitive, and to be at the forefront of technology.

(iii) As the consumer electronics industry is experiencing lacklustre demand, caution must be exercised when Singapore investors wish to move into this subsector.

China is not only an inexpensive export base but also provides the potential of a huge domestic market. According to the contours of government planning, China's share of world electronics exports is expected to increase from the current 0.2 to 2% by the end of the century. Hence, the future of the industry remains bright and the main thrust behind future economic growth is expected to be led by the component and industrial electronics subsectors.

REFERENCES

"China and Mongolia", *Economist Intelligent Unit Country Report,* Arthur Andersen, 1st Quarter 1994.

Economic Survey of Singapore, Department of Statistics, Singapore, 1993.

"Foreign Investment in the PRC 1991–92", *Jetro China Newsletter,* No. 102, January–February 1993.

Survey of Singapore's Investment Abroad 1990, Department of Statistics, Singapore.

Tam-Sun Yue Duk, "China's Expanding Consumer Market: Business Opportunities for Singapore Firms", *Singapore Briefing,* DBS Bank, April 1993.

United Nations Industrial Development Organisation, "China: Towards Sustainable Industrial Growth" in *Industrial Development Review Series.* Blackwell Publishers Inc., Oxford, 1992.

FORMS OF BUSINESS

Chapter 9

The Choice of Relevant Investment Forms in China: Wholly Foreign-owned Versus Joint Venture Enterprises

BY
WONG Wei
LEE See Tin
THOO Kah Fah
TANG Y.Q.

INTRODUCTION

THE PEOPLE'S REPUBLIC of China was founded in 1949 when Mao Zedong led the Chinese Communist Party to victory over the Kuomintang. An economic modernisation programme was implemented and by 1956, nearly all of the country's commercial and manufacturing enterprises had become state-owned. This was followed by a ten-year period of Cultural Revolution from 1985 to 1995. A new era arose in the 1970s after trade relations were established with the United States. There was a rapid increase in China's trade with the United States.

When Deng Xiaoping took over the reins in 1977, he continued with bolder economic reforms. His position weakened in the aftermath of the Tiananmen Square massacre in June 1989. However, in early 1992, he reemerged to launch an aggressive open door policy. China's trade relations with the United

States have been characterised by rows over trade, human rights and arms proliferation. Her relationship with the United Kingdom worsened in the row over Hong Kong. China then turned to the ASEAN countries for trade. In 1990, Indonesia agreed to re-establish relations with China after 23 years of estrangement. Singapore followed suit.

From 1979 to 1991, total foreign direct investments in China were US$52.3 billion. During this period, 42,027 joint ventures with Chinese foreign capital, exclusive foreign investment, and co-operative forms were set up. This chapter attempts to give potential investors an insight into the two forms of investments in China, namely the foreign-Chinese joint venture and the wholly foreign-owned enterprise with a specific emphasis on two major cities in the Sichuan province – Chengdu and Chongqing.

Materials, statistics and information on the various forms of investments in China were gathered from newspapers, libraries, and various articles. Valuable information and feedback were also collected in the seminars and meeting sessions hosted by municipal government officials, academicians and state-owned and privately owned enterprises during the Business Mission. In addition, group discussions and direct interviews were conducted with selected officials to get their views on the best forms of investment.

FORMS OF INVESTMENT

There are many forms of investment in China which can include an equity or contractual joint venture, a wholly foreign-owned enterprise, a processing and assembly plant, a representative office, a branch of a foreign company, or simply the investment in B shares. The two more popular forms of investment are foreign-Chinese joint ventures and wholly foreign-owned enterprises. Co-operative or contractual joint ventures are less popular because there is no legal protection for the foreign investor because it is of unlimited liability. We will therefore examine two main forms: the wholly foreign-owned enterprise and the foreign-Chinese joint venture.

Prior to 1 January 1994, there was differentiation in the treatment of wholly owned foreign investment and foreign-Chinese joint venture. For example, for 100% foreign ownership, projects must not require state assistance or state-distributed raw materials. Projects also cannot produce items for domestic sales that are subject to distribution restriction or, for exports, items that require an export licence. On the other hand, negotiations with the Chinese partners over the joint venture contracts can take a long time.

With the liberalisation of rules and regulations governing the different forms of investment, and the unification of the dual exchange rate system and the abolishment of Foreign Exchange Certificate in January 1994, there is now little differentiation between the two forms of investment from the viewpoint of taxation and legislation. The question therefore arises as to which form of investment in China the investor should choose.

CHARACTERISTICS OF FOREIGN-CHINESE JOINT VENTURE AND WHOLLY FOREIGN-OWNED FIRMS

A foreign-Chinese joint venture is basically a partnership between the Chinese and the foreign investors. On 1 July 1979, the Fifth National People's Congress passed the *Law of the People's Republic of China on Chinese Foreign Equity Joint Ventures ("Joint Venture Law")*. This was China's first investment law allowing foreign participation in China's economy. The *Joint Venture Law* established the basis for investing in China through the form of a joint venture which is a structure modelled along the lines of a company with a board of directors, separate legal entity and liability limited to the contributions made by the parties to the joint venture. On 4 July 1990, the *Joint Venture Law* was revised to allow the foreign party to a joint venture to appoint the chairman of the Board of Directors (formerly disallowed under the 1979 *Joint Venture Law*) as well as permitting multiple parties to be participants in a joint venture (Lawrence, 1994).

While local participation is still required in countries such as Indonesia, Malaysia and Thailand, China permits complete foreign ownership of a legal entity in the PRC, provided that such an entity is engaged in activities which involve either technology transfer or export production. As early as 1986, the National People's Congress adopted the law on Wholly Foreign-Owned enterprises to be established within the People's Republic of China making the Chinese legal system in this regard far more liberal than many other jurisdictions in Asia (Lawrence, 1994).

Before the establishment of a joint venture or a wholly foreign-owned enterprise, the parties concerned must submit their project proposal to the relevant authority for approval. Once approved, they will need to conduct a feasibility study on the project. The feasibility study report, together with the Articles of Association and the Joint Venture contract (not required for wholly foreign-owned company) will again be submitted for approval. Upon obtaining the approval certificate, the parties can then proceed to apply for their business registration licence (Chongqing Municipal Government, 1993). The procedures herc are different from Singapore where foreign investors are allowed to establish a new company without having to submit any project proposal or feasibility study report to the Registrar of Companies.

As of 31 December 1993, there were 167,500 foreign-affiliated enterprises in China (*Min Sheng Pao*, 1994). The breakdown is as follows:

Foreign-Chinese joint ventures	107,800	(64%)
Co-operative joint ventures	25,500	(15%)
Wholly foreign-owned enterprises	34,200	(21%)
Total	167,500	

About 80% of these foreign-affiliated companies are concentrated in the economically liberalised coastal regions. They are mostly export-oriented companies which process and assemble parts, then export the majority of the finished products of foreign-affiliated companies with high export ratios which include electronic products, textile products and apparel and footwear (Jetro, 1994). Based on the above statistics, it can be seen that the joint venture is the most preferred form of investment in China by foreign investors.

Similarly, in a report from *The Straits Times* (15 February 1994) of Singapore, out of the 11 public listed companies which have invested in China since January 1994, most have chosen joint ventures as the preferred form of investment. Feedback and opinion of municipal officials, academicians and private investors on the preferred form of investment were also gathered. Municipal officials' views are fairly flexible as far as the two forms of investment are concerned. For strategic projects, the officials preferred a joint venture co-operation of which the government holds controlling interest (Zhang, 1994). From the point of view of academia, there are pros and cons as to both forms of investment (Yang, 1994). The choice, according to them, depends on the investors' preference. The private investors' views tend to be varied depending on their financial strength, possession of superior technology and attractiveness of their investment to the host country.

ADVANTAGES AND DISADVANTAGES OF FOREIGN-CHINESE JOINT VENTURES

The following are some of the advantages and disadvantages of foreign-Chinese joint ventures and wholly foreign-owned enterprises.

Advantages of a Foreign-Chinese Joint Venture

(i) China's traditional political system was fundamentally a pattern of personal relations. Today, personal relations known as *guanxi* form an invisible network which often provides the most expedient way of getting things done (Lawrence, 1994). We have seen many examples of this during this study trip. Examples are:

  (a) The Japan-Chinese JV – Yamaha JV is based on prior ten years of co-operative effort and relationship between Yamaha and the Chinese entity. The *guanxi* with the local authority enabled it to successfully appeal against the proposed construction of a highway across its factory and the approval was given within one and half days.

  (b) The Singapore-Chinese JV – Wearnes Brothers and Huaxin International that develops the Orchard Manor originated from the meeting of minds of two old classmates from the two companies.

(ii) The local partner's intimate knowledge of the domestic market, labour force characteristics, distribution channels, Chinese customs, rules and regulations which are critical for the success of this project.

(iii) Contribution by the local partner in terms of additional capital and/or resource and/or labour skills.

(iv) It is the favoured form of investment by the Government for strategic projects such as the development and/or management of investment in infrastructure where the Government would want to own a controlling share.

(v) In the event of nationalisation due to a change of Government policy (although this appears remote if one looks at the current trend of liberalising the economy in China), joint ventures may be treated on a more favourable manner as local interest is involved.

Disadvantages of a Foreign-Chinese Joint venture

(i) Finding a suitable partner and maintaining a successful relationship is not easy, just like any marriage. A lot can be learned from the Chinese saying "to sleep in the same bed but dream different dreams". Most of the reasons for a breakdown in joint ventures negotiations or break-ups of joint ventures after the deal is sealed is because there are two parties who have decided to get into the same bed with dreams that are fundamentally different (Lawrence, 1994).
(ii) At times it can be extremely difficult and taxing to break-up the joint venture when the foreign investor finds that the relationship is not workable or that the joint venture has failed to fulfil its objectives. The Chinese partner can make it difficult for the foreign partner. For example, it may want an official re-evaluation of the assets to arrive at each party's due share. This evaluation may take very long if one does not have the right relationship with the authority doing the assessment. This will certainly impede the foreign partner from taking its share of the profits/assets and repatriating its earnings to the parent companies.
(iii) In a joint venture, the foreign partner must be prepared to share its technology and, in certain cases, its trade secrets with the local partner. Sometimes this may lead to conflict of interests especially where the local partner also enters into joint ventures with other foreign investors which may be the foreign partner's competitors.
(iv) Foreign companies in a joint venture are subject to certain regulations on their capital contributions. For instance, in the registered capital of a joint venture, the proportion of the investment contributed by the foreign partner shall not be less than 25% in general. There is also a required proportion between the total investment and the registered capital as shown in Table 9-1.

Advantages of a Wholly Foreign-owned Enterprise

(i) Given a choice, most companies would desire a wholly foreign-owned set-up as they would have full autonomy over the operations of the company. They have a say in their investments and whether

TABLE 9-1
Capital Contribution Regulations

Total Investment	Registered capital proportional to total investment
US$3 million and under	70%
(a) US$3 million – 10 million (b) If under US$4.2 million	(a) 50% (b) Not less than US$2.1 million
(a) US$10 million – 30 million (b) If under US$12.5 million	(a) 40% (b) Not less than US$5 million
(a) Over US$30 million (b) If under US$36 million	(a) 33.3% (b) Not less than US$12 million

Source: Publication from China Embassy, 1994

to retain or repatriate profits.

(ii) It facilitates tax planning for the company as the company has full flexibility, for example, in using transfer pricing to minimise its tax liability in its worldwide operations.

(iii) Perhaps the greatest advantage is that it avoids the hassle of having to choose the right partner and the protracted negotiations on the terms and conditions after the partner has been chosen.

(iv) It enables the company to retain or maintain confidentiality over its trade secrets, research findings and technology expertise within the company.

(v) It allows the foreign investors complete flexibility in liquidating and forming new companies, for example, where the original venture is unsuccessful or where the company desires to go into new ventures to gain full tax advantage.

Disadvantages of a Wholly Foreign-owned Enterprise

(i) In the event of change in national policies, such as expropriations or nationalisation, a wholly foreign-owned enterprise is more likely to face unfavourable consequences.

(ii) It faces certain restrictions in the domestic market, especially in investments in strategic projects such as investment in infrastructure developments.

(iii) It may suffer as a result of its lack of knowledge of the local "modus operandi", operations, rules, regulations, workforce characteristics and market distribution channels. These may result in a failed investment.

(iv) It may have difficulty getting projects. Having no *guanxi*, it would have to spend a tremendous amount of time and money creating a relationship with the municipal government to get the proposals or projects approved. The lack of *guanxi* is the greatest handicap and it is often the main reason why foreign investors prefer to enter into joint ventures with a local partner or the government.

SUMMARY AND CONCLUSION

Based on the above mentioned analysis, it can be seen that the joint venture is the most preferred form of business venture in the cases which we have studied during our field trip. The joint venture, as in any form of business, is a marriage of relationships and in order to avoid the early break-up of the marriage, there are certain considerations which have to be observed by the business partners.

As an investor, you must know your capabilities, strengths and weaknesses. Any shortcoming which you have identified should be mitigated or made up by a joint venture partner who possesses the needed expertise. Strategically, the Chinese partner can be looked upon as an "insurance policy" in the venture.

Analyse your prospective partner's contribution to the joint venture in terms of market and share, management and labour relationship, pool of skilled manpower, and their relationship with the local government. It is also important to review the financial reports to check the track record of the partner's company. The information can be obtained or verified from trade associations located locally or in China, site visits to the prospective partner's place of business, or through exchange of information with the partner's trading contacts, competitors and middleman who arranges such business tie-ups.

It is important to have a clear understanding of the Chinese way of doing things, their language, their inclinations and their dislikes. For example, in China "yes" is the start of negotiations (Lawrence, 1994). It means "let sit down and talk seriously". The Chinese are fond of conducting protracted negotiations which in a way is similar to waging a guerrilla war. The rationale is to frustrate the negotiating party with this psychological tactic so that they can achieve an "upper hand" in the deal.

China has developed a legal system from scratch since 1979. This is largely to cater for foreign investors. During the last 14 years, China has undertaken legal reforms which took Europe some five centuries to accomplish. Under these circumstances, a lawyer who is well-versed with Chinese legislation will provide valuable counsel for the business deal. An effective interpreter can moderate a lively two-way communication between the parties concerned. Therefore, when negotiating a business venture in China, it is important to be a good listener and react sensibly without preconceptions as to what the other party has said.

REFERENCES

A Brief Introduction to Suzhou, Publication from Chinese Embassy, 1994.

Brahm Lawrence J., "Doing Business in China", *Asia Business Law Review - No. 4*, April, 1994.

"Foreign Investment in China", *Jetro China Newsletter,* No. 102, 1994.

Guide to Investment of Chongqing Economic & Technological Development Zone, Chongqing Municipal Government, 1993.

Yang Kang, Professor from South West University of Finance & Economics, Business Study Mission Speech, Chengdu, 1994.

Zhang Qi, Deputy Secretary of Chongqing, Business Study Mission Speech, Chongqing, 1994.

Chapter 10

The Choice of Appropriate Partners in China: State-owned Enterprises, Companies or Private Entities

BY
ONG Chong Hien
OW Kong Chung
CHANG Jin Ping

INTRODUCTION

THERE ARE BASICALLY many forms of potential partnerships such as manufacturing joint ventures, sales partner, technical collaboration, licensee, remarketer subcontractor, franchising, etc. For purposes of this chapter, we will narrow our focus to the following associations: a business joint venture partner, a sales and distribution partner (e.g., agency), and a co-operative partner.

The same principle of analysis would apply for any other partnership forms. The foreign company could be a large multinational company (MNC) or a fair-sized Singapore company.

BACKGROUND

China has been receiving increased attention from worldwide business executives, especially in the last few years. In 1993, her GDP was 13.4% despite efforts by the central government to “cool down” the economy. For 1994, her GDP grew at 11.6% while industrial output has risen by a staggering 16.4% in the first four months of 1994. Interest from foreign firms to operate or invest in China is hardly surprising since it is projected that by the turn of the century, China will be the largest market in the world and ahead of the U.S. At the same time, during the recent World Economic Forum at Geneva in April 1994 top executives picked China to be the most competitive nation by the year 2010.

Forming alliances with local partners become part of many foreign companies’ strategic plans in China. Two broad categories of companies are examined in this report; namely the state-owned enterprises and private entities. Our examination reveals that it would be far more comprehensive to re-classify the two broad categories into government enterprises and private enterprises. Within government enterprises, two types of business entities are reviewed: traditional (old-style) state-owned enterprises and government-linked companies. Under private enterprises, two basic groups of entities are reviewed: original private companies and ex-state-owned enterprises.

METHODOLOGY

The group prepared for the business mission by doing some research on related topics before our departure for China. We studied and analysed numerous business newspapers, journals and special China reports. As China is an up-and-coming market, and since many countries have expressed keen interest in investing in China, there are many reports on business ventures and foreign investment in China but most of them do not directly study the choice of partner. Instead, they tend to examine the various types of partnerships or business operators in China. This aspect of our research, however, did provide us with a good perspective of the economic and investment situation in China thereby enabling us to come up with a broad framework for the report.

During the business mission proper, we had the opportunity to attend various seminars and talks delivered by key government officials, university economists and prominent business leaders and managers (who are involved in various forms of business ventures). Through such seminars and interviews, we managed to obtain more up-to-date data and information on some of the reasons for the choice of partners, the problems encountered and future expansion opportunities. We also visited various business ventures and industrial zones to get a first-hand view of business developments in the interior part of China. During such visits, many of the business managers shared their experiences and views of their business ventures with us and we gathered some information from them that could be useful to this particular study. Another useful part of the business mission trip was the opportunity to interact informally with the academic staff and peers who shared their views with us and occasionally pointed us to additional possible sources of information.

THE FOREIGN COMPANY

Before any assessment on the suitability of state enterprises versus private companies as potential partners can be made, one has to first establish the objectives and considerations of the foreign companies who have intentions to invest in China. Some of these would include:

(i) scope of market accessibility, that is, if the products and/or services are intended for exports, domestic nation-wide or domestic regional;
(ii) market penetration, that is, the depth of market share aspired for and whether niche market strategy is employed;
(iii) level of requirement for fast and close support to customers and clients; and
(iv) level of technology and the corresponding human resource required.

TRADITIONAL STATE-OWNED ENTERPRISES

It has always been noted that China has three major problems to address in the midst of her highly geared economic reform programmes. They are high inflation, the growing income disparity between the rich and the poor, and the ailing financial position of the state-owned firms.

In the April 1994 report by the State Statistical Bureau, it was highlighted that 49.6% of China's some 110,000 state-owned firms were in the red in the first quarter this year, a marked increase from 34.2% a year earlier. Losses amounted to 15.7 billion yuan (S$2.6 billion), up by 79.7%. Local Chinese economists believed this figure will be much higher as the accounting system in China has yet to converge with international accounting standards and at least another 30% of state-owned enterprises will also be considered unprofitable if hidden assistance such as cheap government loans and subsidised raw materials are taken into account.

Even Beijing's Shougang Corporation, a model state-owned company which has invested aggressively overseas, needed bank loans to pay wages. As such, the Chinese government intends to auction or lease off the small state-owned enterprises which are defined as those with a workforce of under 1,000 people. It plans to corporatise medium and large state-owned enterprises into shareholding companies and foreign investors will be encouraged to buy the shares of these companies or their subsidiaries.

Generally, most of the country's top technical and management staff work with the state enterprises. There is an abundant pool of staff with strong competencies to embrace new technologies and product development ideas. One reason why state firms are unprofitable is their high employee burden. The iron rice bowl philosophy and free (or very highly subsidised) medical, housing and education benefits are standard obligations of the state-owned firms. Until recently, state-owned companies have had very limited retained earnings and this makes profitable growth opportunities difficult. There has also been a traditional state control on how and where products and services are to be distributed.

State-owned firms vary in organisation size which, in turn, influences the organisational structure. An example of a large (and extensive) state-owned group with the large corporate relationship are the three economic entities that supervise and manage the petroleum industry, namely, the China National Petroleum Corporation (CNPC), the China National Offshore Oil Corporation (CNOOC), and China Petro-Chemical Corporation (SINOPEC). These organisations report to the State Economic and Trade Commission which, in turn, reports to the State Planning Commission.

Each entity (or corporation) has a large number of operating companies under them and the total staff count is several hundred thousands. SINOPEC, for example, has a registered capital of RMB 21 billion, controls 37 subordinate refineries, 21 basic organic chemical plants, 15 synthetic fibre plants, 5 synthetic rubber plants, 3 synthetic resin plants, 8 plastic resin plants and 13 chemical fertiliser plants. Most, if not all, of these companies have vast experience in working with foreign companies. For instance, enterprises under CNPC in 1991 conducted 905 economic contracts with partners from more than 20 countries such as Canada, Peru, Venezuela, Indonesia, India, Papua New Guinea, Russia and others.

The key question related to the topic of this study is whether the financial state and social obligations of the state-owned firms hamper their candidacy as good potential business partners. Or, because these firms are state-owned, does it enhance or lessen their suitability as partners?

GOVERNMENT-LINKED COMPANIES

Government-linked companies (GLCs) are generally less known, partly because they are a relatively newer institutional evolution within China's economic reforms and, also, because some people would prefer to classify GLCs as state-owned. Hence, their identity and character have somehow never taken a prominent profile until the last few years which has seen the explosive growth of GLCs in China.

GLCs may be described as companies that use state-owned capital from their parent units to start up or expand, and where the parent units could be government bodies, public organisations and institutions, or state-owned enterprises (SOEs). This report treats GLCs as different from SOEs[1]; unlike SOEs, GLCs are generally autonomous (free from administrative ties to government bureaucracy), profit-oriented and dynamic entities with little or no administrative roles. Hence, they operate like any commercial enterprise that has to manage its own budget and growth. Interestingly, GLCs typically enjoy the SOE-type advantages like the availability of professional human resources and good *guanxi* networks.

Prominent examples of GLCs would be the International Trust and Investment Corporation (ITIC) enterprises for the central government and nearly every Chinese province (the central government's China ITIC [CITIC] is most well-known and frequently featured owing in part to its

---

1 GLC in this study refers to the "Jingji Shiti" (real economic entities). Other types of organisations that could fall under the definition of GLCs like "Kongjiazi" (empty shells) or "Fanpai Gongsi" (government companies that merely changed names to become business-oriented companies) are not considered in our analysis of partners.

extremely strong branch in Hong Kong). Consider the Guangdong ITIC (GITIC). It has some 6,000 employees involved in everything from fund management to cement manufacturing. The market value of GITIC's assets are estimated at US$5.5 billion and the conglomerate is involved in issuing bonds in international markets, providing funds for infrastructure projects, assisting the privatisation of state enterprises, operating plants that make cement, aluminium, glass, etc., and it operates more than twenty hotels throughout China and has investment projects in U.S., Thailand, Hong Kong and Macau. GITIC also has joint ventures with McDonald's and PPG Industries of the U.S.A. and is aggressively pursuing a partnership with Chrysler.

In considering GLCs as suitable local partners, one has to also understand the deeper nature of GLCs. GLCs recent phenomenal growth and characteristic could well be only part of a transition in China's move towards the open market system. It is still unclear how their role and profile in China's economy will change with time. GLC's ownership and relationships with the government bodies tend to be fairly complicated for foreign firms to fully understand, and one may uncover apparent contradictions within the enterprise structure.

ORIGINAL PRIVATE ENTERPRISES

Original private enterprises tend to be much smaller[2] but more profitable, as compared with the SOEs. Since their objectives are driven by the bottom-line, more prudent financial management is typically exercised. However, most of these private enterprises tend to concentrate in certain specific regional localities and would, of course, have a relatively narrower field of business specialities. But those that exist over the mid and long term tend to be very good and comprehensive both in local network and understanding of their field of speciality. The number of original private firms rose 26% to over 300,000 in 1994 from 238,000 in 1993.

Unlike state-owned enterprises, private enterprises are disadvantaged in several aspects. The latter are subjected to more limited funding opportunities, less government assistance and quite possibly more

[2] The description of "smaller" here refers to the organisation size with respect to the operations in China itself. It does not include the actual conglomerate size overseas considering that many private enterprises are foreign-owned.

"barriers" in establishing an extensive *guanxi* network. Also, China's burgeoning private sector is subjected to crippling levies imposed by local authorities. Besides the regular income tax payments, private businesses in some provinces can be forced to pay at least a hundred other levies imposed by local government departments in the name of improving urban infrastructure, transportation and management, and they often exceed the amount paid in state taxes.

It is noteworthy that many of these private companies are branches of larger foreign-based enterprises, particularly from Hong Kong. A good example of a foreign-based private enterprise operating in China is the New World Development Limited of Hong Kong. The conglomerate is heavily involved in property, transport and construction businesses in China and it is expanding into telecommunications and electronic media. In 1993, the New World conglomerate was ranked 508th under the Business Week Global 1000 listing with a market value of US$7.4 billion. Consider that before the year 2000, the group's investment assets deployed in China will be about 25%!

As with many private enterprises, New World operates predominantly in the booming coastal areas though it is making important inroads into China's internal regions. Basically, as with most successful private enterprises in China, New World management spent much of the initial years building up *guanxi* and recognising that a developed *guanxi* can make up for the lack of rules of industrial laws.

The private enterprises ability to be good in their respective field of business and financial management skills make them stable potential partners. However, depending on the foreign company's interest, their relatively less extensive structure, both in organisation and *guanxi*, may limit their usefulness as a local partner. This, however, can be overcome in part if the private enterprise's parent company is large and strong.

EX-STATE-OWNED ENTERPRISES

Ex-state-owned enterprises (Ex-SOEs) are former state-owned companies that were sold off or converted into shareholding companies. At the end of 1993, 4,000 state-owned companies became stockholding entities, but of these, fewer than 200 companies are listed on China's two main exchanges. These enterprises are driven by bottom-line objectives and since they were once state-owned, their previous *guanxi* network and existing core technical/production staff skills are still retained in the "new" companies. Welfare support and maintenance staff are theoretically not part of the latter.

An excellent example of such a converted private enterprise is the Yizheng Chemical Fiber Company located some forty miles north-east of Nanjing. Yizheng is the seventh of China's famous First Nine state companies to be sold partially to the public and it began in March, 1994, with the Stock Exchange of Hong Kong listing of US$300 million (a 29.4% stake). The company is one of the leanest and best performing of the First Nine. Yizheng's management was picked from the cream of China's chemicals industry and technical universities. Equipped with its own wharf and barges, the company is the fifth largest polyester manufacturer in the world. Yizheng's technology is also among the newest in China, considering that the company's actual operations started only in 1984.

The original Yizheng has some 20,000 workers but after the listing, one of the biggest headaches was figuring out what to do with workers who were not directly involved in production (teachers, store clerks, waitresses, sweepers, doormen, etc.). The company tried to transfer many of the 7,000 non-production workers into the unlisted portion but even then it was not easy. As with all privatising SOEs, the most difficult part of the listing process was to separate out the non-listed part.

The advantages of having ex-SOEs as partners are clearly evident. Again, it would be in the foreign firm's interest if they appreciate the fairly emotional process of transition that the ex-SOEs' management and workers are going through (since the privatisation process itself is a relatively recent phenomenon). While the social obligations of ex-SOEs are technically divorced from them, reality suggests that the procedure is not so straightforward. Still, the resources and extensive *guanxi* of ex-SOEs place them in a favourable position to be considered as a partner depending on the business association.

SUMMARY AND CONCLUSION

In a joint venture partnership, most foreign companies, in particular MNCs, are seeking a production base to produce their products at a much cheaper cost for the Chinese domestic market and possibly also for the export market. Clearly, quality management becomes key in these manufacturing set-ups and the more sophisticated the technology, the more critical is the presence of experienced technical staff. Joint venture manufacturing can be very complex. The need for *guanxi*, both during the formative stage and after the joint venture manufacturing company is in operation, is crucial to the long term health of the joint venture. In these respects, the GLCs and ex-SOEs become the clear potential partner of choice. SOEs can be seriously considered so long as the state-owned would-be partner provides its portion of the funding and resources to the joint venture (regardless of its own financial state). The joint venture would typically be run as an independent company and, hence, there are very limited expectations bearing on it from the local parent's financial health.

GLCs and ex-SOEs operate on a different platform (bottom-line objectives) as compared with state-owned companies but they retain the staff strengths/resources and important *guanxi* network. Negotiations with them are relatively simpler since there is a more common frame of mind.

For a sales-cum-distribution partnership (principal and agent), there is arguably much flexibility in the choice of partners. This is basically a business association for targeted sales and distribution goals. However, state-owned companies and former state-owned companies would typically have little interest in such relationships as these are low value-added to them. Also, the private enterprises would be the ones with greater sales and commercial experiences and these are the ones that would be willing to become agents. In such cases, the challenge would be to find the right private enterprise to form a business association. Not surprisingly, many large MNCs that are looking at some sales-cum-distribution strategy in China find it more worthwhile to set up their own wholly-owned sale office(s) in China.

In the case of co-operative partnerships, the SOEs stand out as the strongest candidates for potential partnerships. Most of these partnerships stem from joint technology development, or even technical transfer programmes, that ensures product and service sales for the foreign firm. The association between foreign and local companies are supported by motivations beyond solely commercial profit objectives. Government support and "hard" incentives are important and, hence, the preference of SOEs as a first choice. GLCs, too, could be considered for similar reasons.

REFERENCES

"Ailing State Firms Hamper China's Anti-Inflation Plans", *Business Times*, 18 April 1994.

"China's Industrial Output Grows 16 Percent, Prompting Calls to Curb Inflation", *Business Times*, 18 May 1994.

"China Re-Organises Oil and Gas Administration", *Hydrocarbon Asia*, July/August 1993.

"China Urged to Protect Private Sector from Crippling Levies", *Business Times*, 25 April 1994.

Delilkhan Gerald A., "New World's China Thrust", *Silkwinds Portrait Feature*, July/August 1994.

"Executives Pick China as Most Competitive Nation in 2010", *Business Times*, 21 April 1994.

Goh Keng Swee, "The Phenomenon that is the Chinese TVE", *Business Times*, 19 May 1994 (China Summit Meeting, Beijing, May 1994).

Hirsh Michael, "China: Anatomy of a Privatisation", *Institutional Investor,* April 1994.

Lee Schutz, "China's 13.4 Percent GDP Growth Better than Better", *Business Times*, April 1994.

"Many Chinese State Firms Unable to Pay Workers", *Business Times*, 25 April 1994.

"Red Capitalist: Inside World of China's Hottest Dealmaker", *Business Week*, 9 May 1994.

Wong John and Chen Kang, *The Growth of Government-linked Companies in China. A Solution Or a Problem for Reform*? National University of Singapore, 1994.

Yong Pow Ang, "Good Deals to be Had as China Divests State Enterprises", *The Straits Times*, 6 April 1994.

CASE STUDIES

Chapter 11

Puyi-Briggs and Stratton Engine Corporation: Case Study of a China-U.S. Joint Venture

BY
LIM Yan Tim
Patrick FOK
Man Keen

INTRODUCTION

IN 1980, THE U.S. granted China the Most Favoured Nation (MFN) status. The United States' renewal of the MFN trading status of China in June 1994 underpins the importance of China as a trading partner to the business sector in the United States. To sustain its competitiveness in the world, the U.S. needs to align a partnership with China and build a long-term competitive position in a region that includes the most competitive of nations – Japan.

During the Business Study Mission to Chengdu, Chongqing and Wuhan, we had the opportunity to visit a joint venture (JV) set up by Chinese and U.S. partners, namely, the Puyi-Briggs & Stratton Engine Corporation (abbreviated as PBS in this case study) located at 20 Erlang Road, Shiqiaopu, Chongqing. We toured the factory and held brief discussions with both the Chinese and U.S. partners. The visit enlightened us on several aspects of setting up JVs in China, namely: (1) the motivating factors for both parties in setting up JVs in the Sichuan area; (2) the problems that could be encountered in such JVs; (3) how such problems were resolved or could be resolved; and (4) critical success factors (CSFs) for China-U.S. JVs.

The PBS forms the subject of this chapter. The primary objective of the case study is to identify the CSFs for China-U.S. JVs in the Sichuan area. The identification of CSFs might assist U.S. (or other foreign companies) and Chinese companies in performing feasibility studies on setting up JVs in the Sichuan area. Other secondary objectives include listing the motivating factors for such JVs and highlighting problems that could be encountered. A comparison is also made between China-U.S. JVs and China-Japan JVs, as Japan is China's top trading partner.

BACKGROUND

Foreign Investment in China

From 1980 to 1989, the proportion of Sino-foreign JVs and wholly foreign-owned ventures jumped only marginally from 0.5% to 3.5%. However, starting from the second half of 1990, and especially in 1991 and 1992, China experienced its third foreign investment boom — one far greater and more sustained than the previous two boom years of 1985 and 1988. A breakdown by type of investment during this period revealed a surge in JVs and contractual JVs which had been sluggish in growth compared with wholly foreign-owned companies in recent years.

In the first half of 1993, the number of JVs with foreign capital rose above 120,000 and probably surpassed 150,000 for the year as a whole. They are fast reaching the tenth percentile level of China's GNP. Foreign ventures now account for 20% of all China's exports and 30% of its imports. In 1993, the U.S. was ranked third in China's top trading partners.

The surge in JVs and contractual JVs is believed to be attributable to several factors during the domestic business recovery in China: (1) there was a succession of large JV projects that were restarted; (2) the shortage of funds in domestic companies had eased; and (3) attention had once again focused on the massive size of the Chinese market. The result was that the merits of JVs and contractual JVs which are allowed to sell a portion of their production in the domestic market were reevaluated as compared to wholly foreign-owned companies which, in principle, are obliged to export all of their products.

Foreign Investment in Sichuan Area

Since 1992, when the central government granted Chengdu and Chongqing open coastal city status (the right to offer tax and investment incentives), the two cities have attracted large amounts of foreign investment. Between 1992 and 1993, the value of contracted foreign investment in Sichuan practically tripled to US$2.4 billion and most of it was in Chengdu and Chongqing.

According to the Deputy Director of Foreign Trade in Chongqing, there are 1,470 foreign investment firms in Chongqing as of May 1994, and 890 (60%) are JVs. This fact highlights the importance of JVs in the Sichuan area and the relevance of this case study to foreign companies, especially U.S. companies which are planning to establish JVs in China.

METHODOLOGY

This report discusses some of the crucial issues that U.S. and Chinese JV partners should consider prior to setting up operations in China. The CSFs identified are obtained from the case study of a China-U.S. JV, namely PBS.

The information that is contained in this report comes from three sources, namely: (1) preliminary information gathering prior to the trip (details of the reference materials used can be found in the references); (2) a factory tour at PBS on 15 June 1994; and (3) discussion sessions with Mr. Li Run Nian, Plant General Manager, and Mr. Brown, VP (Briggs & Stratton, U.S.A.).

STRATEGIC ATTRIBUTES

Background Information on PBS

Mr. Xiao Yang, the governor of Sichuan and former Mayor of Chongqing, visited the Milwaukee headquarters of Briggs & Stratton in 1986 and had a dialogue with the CEO during which he invited Briggs & Stratton to invest in the city of Chongqing. Soon after, the contract between Puyi and Briggs & Stratton was signed. The JV, which manufactures and sells small gasoline engines (10 hp and 16 hp), took one year to start production.

Investment in the JV amounted to US$7 million. The U.S. side has a 52% stake in the JV while the Chinese side, consisting of two parties, has a 48% stake. The U.S. investment in the JV consists principally of: (1) equipment imported from the U.S.; and (2) the transfer of skills and technology to the Chinese partner. The Chinese partners, on the other hand, provided the land and buildings for the production of engine parts and the assembly of about 20 different types of products such as lawn mowers, outboard motors, etc. Only 60% of the engine parts are manufactured in Chongqing, using raw materials from the Sichuan area. The remaining 40% are imported from 44 U.S. companies.

The JV is export-oriented as 80% of its engines are exported to overseas markets such as the Philippines, Malaysia, etc. Production has improved dramatically from 500 units exported in 1987 to 20,000 units exported in 1993.

We were informed that the JV registered a RMB 68 million turnover and a RMB 20 million profit before tax in 1993. According to Mr. Li, the superb performance was due largely to efficient factory workers. He noted that the JV obtained a score of 410 in 1993 when measured against an Economic Efficiency Index (norm = 100). Other ratios cited included an impressive profit/fixed asset ratio of 31% and sales/worker of RMB 300,000 in 1993.

The JV currently employs about 144 staff (factory workers, middle management and top management) from the Sichuan area. The factory workers are paid a monthly gross salary of RMB 700, or more than twice the average salary of RMB 300 in the Sichuan province. Middle and top management are paid more than RMB 1,000.

The JV comprises six departments, an office and two workshops. One of the workshops is used for: (1) the receipt, inspection, storage of imported engine parts; (2) the domestic production of certain engine parts such as the die-cast for crankshafts; and (3) the assembly of gasoline engines and packaging. The other workshop is used exclusively for the machining of parts such as the gasoline cylinder, crankshaft and crankshaft gear imported from the U.S.

TQM (Total Quality Management) has been implemented to ensure that gasoline engines produced meet U.S. head office requirements. Each worker is directly responsible for the quality of the part under his charge. In addition, a QC (Quality Control) inspector has been employed to examine the quality of assembled engines prior to packaging.

During the discussion session, we noted that Mr. Li Run Nian had a translator beside him. The translator was interpreting Mr. Brown's speech to Mr. Li Run Nian. Having a translator helps to bridge the communication gap between both partners. Effective communication between both partners can also lead to a more efficient technology transfer process.

Motivating Factors for the JV

The principal motivating factor for setting up the PBS JV was the close link or *guanxi* between the Mayor of Chongqing and the CEO of Briggs & Stratton. This link was forged during the Mayor's visit to Milwaukee and virtually paved the way for a successful JV in Chongqing.

There are also several other motivating factors for setting up U.S.-China (or foreign-China) JVs in the Sichuan area. One of the key advantages offered by Sichuan to foreign investors is access to the domestic market. Because of the demand generated by 110 million consumers, and the difficulty of delivering to the province's remote interior, a larger percentage of products manufactured by foreign enterprises in Sichuan are permitted to be marketed locally. On the coast, as a general rule, 70% of the goods produced by foreign-invested ventures must be exported. Sino-foreign ventures in Sichuan, however, can sell up to 100% of their wares to the domestic market. Moreover, setting up in one of Sichuan's zones enables companies to take advantage of ready infrastructure and lower taxes.

In terms of China's regional development policy, great strides are being made in opening up all regions economically. Considerable authority over foreign investment is being passed on to the local government. For example, Chongqing has the right to approve Sino-foreign joint enterprises. It also has the right to grant export quotas and import licences within the scope authorised by the Ministry of Foreign Economic Relation and Trade. The Sichuan area is rich in minerals and raw materials. Chongqing itself is more than self-sufficient in primary energy and is the outlet of a land-water-railway coordinated transport network in the south-west of China.

The Chinese domestic market may be limited because of the amount of disposable income. The U.S. domestic market may be limited by the size of its population relative to that of China. A JV may enable both partners to scale world markets. The U.S. company could gain a competitive advantage through lower costs of production in China. For example, the supply of labour in the Sichuan area is plentiful and relatively cheap. The U.S. partner minimises the risk of exposing itself to long-term investment capital in China as the Chinese partner would contribute its share of land and working capital. The U.S. partner would benefit from a JV as the Chinese partner: (1) has a better knowledge of local regulations, culture, etc.; (2) can provide the U.S. partner with a competitive edge over other rivals in infrastructure projects; and (3) "insures" the U.S. investment in times of uncertainties. On the other hand, the Chinese partner can gain access to foreign markets through the JV or acquire new skills and technology.

Problems Faced by PBS During Startup

According to Mr. Brown, PBS encountered several problems during its startup phase. The most notable problem was the difficulty in transferring production technology to the Chinese workers. Apparently, proper production procedures were not observed in the workshops which resulted in the production of defective gasoline engines. Moreover, weak inventory controls meant that precious time was spent locating engine parts.

Secondly, the equipment brought in from the U.S. was about 30 to 40 years old and needed to be re-worked to suit PBS's requirements. The JV team encountered numerous problems in maintaining and repairing these machines as the machine specifications or drawings were not well-drawn and, consequently, were difficult to interpret. They also experienced great difficulty in locating spare parts.

Thirdly, an assessment of the quality of engines produced shortly after the startup phase revealed that the engines failed to meet U.S. head office quality standards.

Fourthly, the JV found that it was getting less financially viable to continue importing engine parts from overseas companies. By sourcing for components within China, PBS could circumvent the cost of purchasing, shipping and tariffs associated with importing supplies as well as exorbitant customs duties.

How PBS Solved its Problems

The U.S. partner exercised patience in imparting to the Chinese factory workers the proper sequence of production steps that had to be observed in the manufacture of gasoline engines. They were supportive co-workers who spent a large portion of their time training the Chinese in manufacturing procedures (i.e., machine operation, quality checks, etc.).

PBS implemented TQM to raise the quality of the engines produced. As a result, a second assessment carried out in the last three years confirmed that the quality of the Chinese engines was comparable to those produced in U.S. plants. However, during our factory tour, we noted that some safety regulations were not observed. For example, we were informed that national safety regulation requires workers to put on ear-plugs once the noise level exceeds 84 decibels. Some workers did not comply with this regulation even though the noise level was above 84 decibels.

To avoid having to import engine parts from overseas companies, PBS started to source for a good alternative supplier base of components in Chongqing. It set up a supplier qualification process to identify reliable partners who charged reasonable prices. China encourages local sourcing by joint ventures and wholly foreign-owned enterprises because it usually entails the technological upgrading of local suppliers by the foreign partner, thus enhancing the export potential of the relevant manufacturing sector in China. However, there may be hidden costs in local sourcing. Often, foreign firms must upgrade components to foreign standards by injecting additional investment and equipment into supplying factories. Such upgrading processes may involve huge investments of time, energy, and money.

PBS also intends to perform market studies to determine if there is any domestic demand for a particular type of gasoline engine. If so, it would take advantage of the huge domestic market in Sichuan and less stringent regulations in the Sichuan area to manufacture and market such engines. The market knowledge possessed by the Chinese partner would be invaluable in estimating the market potential of a product in specific areas of China. This export-oriented JV would then eventually become an important penetration point into China's domestic market.

DISCUSSION

Our discussions with Mr. Li and Mr. Brown have enabled us to identify the following CSFs for China-U.S. JVs:

(i) ***The JV should have the right management staff and the right training methods:*** JV management cannot be founded on western management concepts or corporate strategy at the outset. The Chinese factory may be unprepared for standard management methods and foreign techniques. It is also difficult to find U.S. managers with a cross-cultural and cosmopolitan outlook who have a working knowledge and understanding of business practices and customs in China. PBS relied heavily on its Chinese partners who understood Chinese business practices better. Briggs & Stratton also exercised great patience in transferring the correct production techniques to the Chinese. The key to success seems to be in the creation of a management structure that promotes integration of operational systems and takes into consideration the cultural characteristics of Chinese and Western enterprises.

(ii) ***There should be strong support from the municipal government:*** All kinds of businesses in China, whether they are foreign-owned, co-operatives or JVs, would be extremely profitable if they received strong backing from the municipal government. In other words, there should be a strong *guanxi* between the municipal government and the foreign investor. This was opined time and time again during our discussions with foreign investors during the trip.

(iii) ***The Chinese partner must be reliable:*** The choice of one's partner can make or break a deal. Briggs & Stratton had a reliable partner who helped them oversee daily operations and monitor the quality of engines produced, etc. U.S. companies which desire to set up JVs in China should seek reliable Chinese partners by enlisting, for example, the help of the municipal government. Choosing the right Chinese partner also helps in the management of political risk. This is especially so in the face of fast-changing, unpredictable laws and regulatory policies affecting one's investments.

(iv) ***U.S. partner must be supportive of the venture:*** Mr. Li stressed the importance of support from Briggs & Stratton, especially during the startup phase when numerous problems were encountered. Tsuneo Kobayashi, Manager — China Division of Kanebo Ltd. (a China-Japan JV), also stressed that Kanebo had to demonstrate its commitment to play a direct part in the development of China by contributing to the improvement of its level of business management and technology. They worked with a spirit of cooperation among equals. He also mentioned that the foreign partner should make an effort to listen to and understand what the Chinese side has to say.

(v) ***Provide benefits/incentives to retain staff:*** Mr. Li revealed that numerous benefits and incentives were given to the staff. This is reflected in their high salaries and morale. Tsuneo Kobayashi also noted that a venture's performance should be immediately reflected in the workers' salaries. This would result in higher worker morale and higher efficiency.

(vi) ***Perform feasibility study:*** According to the Deputy Secretary-General of Chongqing, foreign investors should choose the right industrial sector to invest in, perform a feasibility study and understand Chinese laws and regulations before setting up JVs. Only then will they have a good chance of succeeding.

COMPARISON BETWEEN CHINA-U.S. JOINT VENTURE AND CHINA-JAPAN JOINT VENTURE

It is well-known that Japan has the largest market share of the China market. The Japanese dominate the China market for reasons other than their obvious geographic proximity to China. Their domination has been cultivated over a long history of dialogue between Japanese executives and the trade officials of China. The continuous, albeit uneven, contact of Japanese firms with China since 1949 has afforded them a considerable head start over U.S. firms.

Japanese firms, in concert with the Japanese government, have been keen to lay the foundation for a long-term relationship with China through the Long-Term Trade Agreement and the 1978 Treaty of Peace and Friendship. The Japanese approach to China places great value on creating continuity and mutual trust in political and commercial dealings. Long-term commercial relationships based on mutual benefit may be valued relatively more by Japan than by western countries. One of the ramifications of this approach is that Japanese executives are able to negotiate more effectively within the Chinese environment because they possess the patience and understanding to influence Chinese group decision-making. Japanese representatives are also well-prepared to deal with China's bureaucracy and management style. To put the U.S. at a further disadvantage, China is also very interested in emulating, in part, the Japanese style of economic organisation. In one Japanese JV, Zhenshe-Yamaha Ltd., the China representative learned to speak Japanese and adopted the Japanese gesture of greeting with a deep and proper Japanese bow. In China, the Chinese are not in favour of western individualism, but are more in favour of group consensus. Therefore, U.S. firms must dedicate more time and energy to training company people to work within a culturally foreign environment.

In general, Japanese firms concede short-term profits in exchange for the long-term benefit of a presence in the China market. Japanese firms also station more people for a longer period of time in order to wait out dilatory negotiations and build personal friendships and trust among counterparts. One often hears the Chinese complain that while U.S. business people stay a few months and then leave, the Japanese remain in the country indefinitely.

U.S. firms are slower in their technology transfer than Japan. Japan offers a level of technology which is easily assimilated. This may be because the Japanese can communicate more effectively, they have done their homework better and understand the Chinese factory's situation better. In PBS, the machines are 30 to 40 years old whereas in ZY, the machines and equipment are technologically more advanced than PBS's machines. In PBS, the U.S. partner experienced difficulty transferring production technology to the Chinese workers during the startup phase. They finally achieved acceptable quality in the last three years.

As reported in the ZY case study, it was observed that the workers understood their tasks, operated the machines skilfully and appeared to be well-trained even though ZY only had a short history of about seventeen months. One may argue that PBS wanted to minimise political risk by keeping its investment commitment low. However, this may be viewed as a lack of commitment by the Chinese. Another argument would be that the Chinese partner may find it difficult to operate highly sophisticated machines. Heavy losses may be incurred should the equipment be damaged by workers who are not appropriately trained. However, this did not happen in ZY. One must therefore not underestimate China's technology assimilation capabilities.

Japanese successes in China could make it difficult for U.S. firms to significantly expand their activities in the future. It is therefore important for the U.S. to respond to opportunities in China, develop its competitiveness and forge closer working links with their Chinese partners.

SUMMARY AND CONCLUSION

The primary objective of this case study was to identify the critical success factors for China-U.S. JVs in the Sichuan area. Secondary objectives included the motivating factors for such JVs and highlighting problems that could be encountered in such JVs.

In summary, the main critical success factors for a China-U.S. JV in the Sichuan area are: (1) the JV should have the right management staff and the right training methods; (2) there should be strong support from the municipal government; (3) the Chinese partner must be reliable; (4) the U.S. partner must be supportive of the venture; (5) the JV should provide adequate benefits/incentives to retain staff; and (6) the U.S. partner should perform a feasibility study.

Further case studies of China-U.S. JVs should be carried out in other parts of China, for example the coastal cities, to ascertain if there are critical success factors and if the ones identified in this chapter are specific to the Sichuan area.

REFERENCES

"China Data", *The China Business Review*, March 1994, pp. 58–9.

Engholm Christopher, *The China Venture: America's Corporate Encounter with the People's Republic of China,* Scott, Foresman and Company, 1989.

"Foreign Investment in the PRC, 1991–92", Jetro, China-North Asia Section, *Jetro China Newsletter*, No. 102, 1993, pp. 16–21.

Kobayashi Tsuneo, "Kanebo's Joint Venture in China", *Jetro China Newsletter*, No. 109, 1993, pp. 2–9, 20.

"Regional Development", *Business China*, 1994, pp. 8–9.

Yeo H. H. Gillian, Hwang S. C., Lee S. P. Eddie, Tan W. L., Tan T. M. and Wong Y. W. Adrian, "Globalisation — What this Means to Companies in Singapore", *Singapore Accountant*, March 1993, pp. 21–30.

Zheng Lu, "China's Economic Reform and Development: Historical Review and Future Prospects", *Economic Reform and Internationalisation: China and the Pacific Region,* Allen and Unwin, 1992, pp. 38–48.

Chapter 12

Case Study of a China-Japan Joint Venture

BY
CHIN Heng Ee
KU Kay Mok

INTRODUCTION

IN RECENT YEARS, China has become a very attractive country for foreign investment activities with her adoption of an open door policy. Some of the factors which appeal greatly to investors are the rich abundance of natural resources such as land, water, agricultural products, minerals and metals, and inexpensive labour.

During the initial period, many of the investments went to the special economic zones (i.e., SEZs) such as Shenzhen. The economic experiments in these SEZs proved to be successful and beneficial to the Chinese economy. In view of this, the inland areas such as Sichuan province were also opened for foreign investments and commercial activities.

Investments and the setting up of foreign commercial enterprises are a recent endeavour in the inland areas. Chinese officials and businessmen in these provinces are not as experienced as their counterparts in the SEZs. Thus, foreign companies and individuals interested in shaping the economies of these inland areas may encounter difficulties.

This report presents a case study of a

Chinese-Japanese joint venture, Jianshe-Yamaha Ltd., which is a manufacturing plant specialising in the production of motorcycles.

BACKGROUND

The Joint Venture Enterprise

Under the existing framework, there are three types of foreign enterprises. They are joint ventures (JV), wholly foreign-owned, and collaborative enterprises.

In a JV enterprise, a Chinese partner teams up with a foreign partner to set up a new enterprise or company. Both parties may contribute capital and assume shares in the JV enterprise. The proportion of shares held indicates the degree of influence of each partner in the management of the JV enterprise.

The main advantage of a JV is the knowledge and contacts of the Chinese partner. A knowledgeable and well-connected partner can smooth many difficulties. For example, when new laws are introduced or existing laws amended by the municipal or central government, a capable and effective Chinese partner can anticipate these laws, and take actions to nullify the ill-effects or take advantage of the new provisions. This ability to adapt quickly to changes in the host country is of critical importance when doing business.

The Jianshe-Yamaha Ltd

This enterprise is a JV between a Chinese firm, Chongqing Jianshe and a Japanese firm, Yamaha Co. It is located in Chongqing city, Sichuan province. The JV was approved on 9 December 1992. It has a registered capital of US$75 million and a total of US$64 million had been injected into the enterprise. Each party has a 50% stake in the JV.

The enterprise owns a total land area of 82,000 square metres with a built-up area of 40,000 square metres. The JV enterprise is a manufacturing plant producing Yamaha motorcycles.

METHODOLOGY

The primary source of information was obtained from a formal presentation given by a Chinese representative from Chongqing-Yamaha Ltd. during a factory visit. The presentation was for members of the NTU MBA Business Study Mission group.

A factory tour was conducted immediately after the presentation. The information disclosed during the presentation and the observations from the factory tour provided interesting insights.

This case study attempts to understand some of the following issues:

(i) What are the benefits for both partners in a JV in China?
(ii) How important is *guanxi* (i.e. relationship) in doing business in China?
(iii) What support is given by the local government?
(iv) What are the difficulties encountered arising from differences in management beliefs and culture?
(v) What are the intangible effects on both partners?

INFORMATION AND OBSERVATIONS

The presentation and the interview session with the Chinese representative revealed the following:

(i) Approval for the Chongqing-Yamaha JV was given on 9 December 1992.
(ii) The total registered capital was US$75 million. The paid-up capital was US$64 million.
(iii) Approximately 90% of the plant and equipment were contributed by the Japanese partners.
(iv) Each partner had a 50% equity.
(v) It has been 17 months since the JV was approved.
(vi) Approximately five days were needed to prepare the application.
(vii) Approval for the joint venture was given approximately one week after the application.
(viii) Construction of the buildings was completed in nine months.
(ix) The manufacturing facilities utilised the old factory of the Chinese partner, Chongqing Jianshe. Consequently infrastructure support such as electricity and water was immediately available.
(x) The manufacturing facilities had just been set up and the factory

was ready to go into production.

(xi) The JV had received strong support from the Chongqing government.

(xii) A request to divert a highway which would have passed through the land owned by the JV was approved by the Chongqing government in only two days.

(xiii) Prior to the JV, the Chinese and Japanese partners had a ten-year working relationship.

(xiv) The General Manager of Norinco (China Northern Industrial Co.), the parent of Chongqing Jianshe, had been to Japan ten years before and entered into a working relationship with Yamaha. The result was an agreement in technology co-operation which had lasted ten years.

(xv) Management of the JV included both Chinese and Japanese nationals. The workers were recruited locally from Chongqing.

(xvi) Management in the JV comprised:

(a) The Chairman (Chinese);
(b) The General Manager (Japanese);
(c) Two deputy general managers (Chinese); and
(d) One deputy general manager (Japanese)

In addition, there were four manufacturing divisions, each headed by a Chinese and a Japanese manager.

(xvii) The average monthly salary for a production worker was RMB 600.

(xviii) The major aim in setting up the JV was to tap the Chinese domestic market. Currently, 6 out of 1,000 people owned a motorcycle. The targeted ownership was 40 out of 1,000 people.

(xix) The technology for the production came from Yamaha. The management system combined both Chinese and Japanese styles.

(xx) The factory owned by the Chinese partner, Chongqing Jianshe, also produced motorcycles of a different make and model. The representative insisted that there was no competition between the Chinese partner and the JV enterprise. The two factories had a commercial relationship and the JV enterprise must pay for any service provided by Chongqing Jianshe.

(xxi) The spare parts and components required for production came from both local and overseas suppliers. However, the percentage of supply was a trade secret.

(xxii) Selection of suppliers was based on price and quality of the parts and components. Nationality of the supplier was not an issue.

(xxiii)The JV enterprise was considered a high-technology venture by the government.

(xxiv)The main obstacle to co-operation between the partners was communication. The representative stressed the need for a Chinese-Japanese translator to eliminate misunderstanding.

DISCUSSION

Analysis of the Joint Venture Relationship

The joint venture between Chongqing Jianshe Company and Yamaha was, in fact, a three-party relationship involving the Jianshe-Yamaha JV, the old Chongqing Jianshe Company and Yamaha. This section of the report enumerates the benefits that each stood to gain from the relationship and some of the prevailing self-interests that provided a counterbalance to the delicate relationship.

The benefits to Yamaha from the relationship were obvious. China was a cheap offshore production centre for Japanese motorcycles. The monthly salary of an average factory worker in the Chinese coastal cities was about RMB 1,000. The salary of the factory workers inland was only one-third of that in the coastal cities. Although the Jianshe-Yamaha JV paid their workers more, at RMB 600, it was still cheap labour for the Japanese.

The Japanese partner also gained a foothold in the potentially huge Chinese market. According to the deputy general manger of Jianshe Yamaha, only 0.6% of the population owned a motorbike. He predicted that this would increase to 4%. In absolute terms that represented 36 million bikes.

The Japanese also found in Chongqing Jianshe a very influential Chinese partner. This was illustrated by the speed at which they were able to persuade the municipal government of Chongqing to divert a planned highway through their property — in barely two days. Dr. Cao Yong, a faculty member in NTU and a former resident of Chongqing city, confirmed that Chongqing-Jianshe's top management had close ties with the municipal government.

The Chinese partner also stood to gain from co-operating with the Japanese. First, there was an infusion of capital and technological investment into the JV. The reforms since 1978 had been concentrated in the coastal cities and only recently had it moved inland. Therefore, the inland cities were hungry for capital and investments.

More importantly, the Chinese benefited from invaluable technological and managerial expertise supplied by the Japanese partner. Such skill transfers in the long run were more important than hard investments in capital and technology. It would equip the Chinese with the capability of participating as international manufacturers in their own right.

Closer analysis provided other insights into the operations of the JV:

(i) ***Export Market***. The Jianshe-Yamaha JV expected to produce 200,000 motorbikes per year at a manufacturer's selling price of RMB 12,000 per motorbike. Assuming a 50% markup, the price that consumers would have to pay was RMB 18,000 per bike. Based on per capita disposable income of RMB 1,500 per year for urban residents in 1991, this was equal to 13 years of income. In view of this, and the fact that some cities in China had legislation to control the motorbike population, much of the production might have to be exported rather than consumed domestically.

(ii) ***Technology Transfer***. Chongqing Jianshe Co. produced about 800,000 motorbikes per year, much of it for the local market. This was estimated to be about 23% of all bikes manufactured in China, a substantial portion of the domestic market. Chongqing Jianshe Co. therefore, had a huge vested interest in the domestic motorbike market. It was a major player and had to modernise its technology in order to maintain its lead in the domestic market; hence, the link-up with Yamaha.

It appeared that the Chinese were leveraging on their huge potential market to entice the Japanese partners to transfer technological and management expertise. On the other hand, the Japanese seem to be carefully controlling and measuring their pace of transferring technology in order to trade for a share of the Chinese market.

With affluence, there was an increasing brand awareness among domestic consumers for bikes such as Yamaha, Honda etc. Thus, the JV was motivated by an element of import-substitution manufacturing. The increasing demand for brand-name bikes from Japan made it unwise for the Chinese authorities to protect the domestic motorbike market from foreign penetration through import barriers. The better alternative was to strike a balance between export-oriented and import-substitution manufacturing by having a joint venture with the Japanese bike makers.

The Commitment of the Chinese and Japanese Partners

A total of US$64 million had been committed. This indicated that both parties were highly committed to make the JV a success.

Importance of *Guanxi* (Relationship)

Guanxi had played an important role, beginning from a working relationship that had started ten years earlier. In the process, a comfortable level of understanding and trust between the two parties was established. It led to the decision of Yamaha Company to select Chongqing Jianshe as its partner in 1992. The decision was significant when one realised that Chongqing Jianshe was located in an inland city rather than in the coastal SEZs.

Support from the Government

Yamaha JV is highly regarded and it is given recognition by the Chongqing government. Consequently, the time taken for various administrative matters was drastically reduced. The government rendered strong support by smoothing administrative requirements and processing applications speedily.

Tax Incentive

Under tax legislation, the JV was required to pay taxes only in the third year after generating profits. (The normal tax rate for foreign-owned – wholly or partially – enterprises was 33%.)

Since the JV enterprise had just begun production, the benefits of the tax incentives had not been realised. But clearly, they were important considerations in the decision-making process.

Supporting Industry and Suppliers

The Chongqing-Yamaha JV needed parts and components for production. Though the JV manager was reticent on this issue, it appeared that a significant portion of the parts was imported.

Japanese companies were generally believed to give preference to Japanese suppliers, even when the price and quality of the parts, compared to those from other suppliers, were less favourable.

The Jianshe-Yamaha representative maintained, however, that such preferential treatment would not arise in the Chinese-Japanese joint venture.

Language and Cultural Differences

According to the Jianshe-Yamaha representative, the greatest obstacle leading to co-operation was communication. The representative emphasised the importance of having a good translator.

It was also observed that the Japanese had been able to introduce some norms into the workplace. For instance, the Chinese representative greeted our delegation with a polite bow. He was also observed to be fluent in Japanese. The manager had adopted some Japanese skills and manners. This behaviour could also be seen in Japanese companies, such as Aiwa Sales Singapore Ltd., in Singapore. Apparently, these measures helped maintain and enhance good working relationships between the two partners.

Management System

The Chinese representative stressed that they had adopted the best of both Chinese and Japanese management systems. However, throughout our tour of the facilities, a strong visual presence of the Japanese management system was evident. For instance, the production floor was very clean, tidy and systematically organised. Production instructions, process explanations and safety signs were seen at many points along the production floor. A section of the production floor was in operation. The workers appeared to understand their tasks and operated the machines skilfully.

Equipment Maintenance and Technology Transfer

The equipment used in the production was technologically sophisticated. The Chinese operators appeared to have been adequately trained to handle the machinery. The machines would also require a maintenance crew of skilled technicians and engineers. It appeared that the Japanese partner was responsible for maintenance and repair. However, in the long run, the Chinese would have to be trained to assume the responsibility.

Quality of the Worker

The workers were skilled and disciplined and appeared to be sufficiently motivated. The prime motivation seemed to be the attractiveness of the factory. Furthermore, the average monthly salary was about RMB 600 which was about twice that of other workers in Chongqing city. The workers also learned skills which would add to their market value.

CONCLUSION

This case study of the Jianshe-Yamaha JV highlighted some important points:

(i) In the short term, the Japanese obtained a cheap source of motorcycle production while in the long-term, they gained access to the Chinese domestic market.
(ii) The Chinese gained both technological and management skills.
(iii) *Guanxi* played an important role in doing business in China.
(iv) The support of the government was vital in all stages of the process from application for approval to operations.
(v) The Japanese management style was dominant.
(vi) The Chinese were quick to adapt and learn new skills and values.

The Jianshe-Yamaha Ltd. was in the beginning phase of operations. Thus, it was too early to predict whether the joint venture would be a success. The results would be clearer in the next three to five years. Nonetheless, with the high degree of commitment from both partners, the chances of success seemed high.

REFERENCES

Itoga Ryo, "Recent Negotiations Over Joint Venture Contracts", *Jetro China Newsletter,* No. 103, March-April 1993.

Kobayashi Tsuneo, "Kanebo's Joint Venture in China", *Jetro China Newsletter,* No. 109, March-April 1993.

The Guide to Investment in Chongqing, Chongqing People's Municipality, 1993.

Watanabe Masumi, "Some Thoughts on Technology Transfer", *Jetro China Newsletter,* No. 103, March–April 1993.

Chapter 13

Feasibility Study on Investment in China*

BY
LEE Suay Wah

INTRODUCTION

Company Profile of Gates Rubber Company

THE GATES RUBBER COMPANY is primarily in the fluid and mechanical power transmission motion control and material transfer business. It manufactures automotive and industrial belts and hose, hydraulic hose, assemblies and connectors for both original equipment manufacturers and replacement markets. Manufacturing, automotive and transportation, construction, agriculture, mining, oil and gas exploration, computer technology and food processing and handling are the primary industries which it serves.

The Gates Rubber Company sells its products through a network of 150,000 distributors, dealers and jobbers worldwide, and directly to automotive and industrial OEMs. It employs more than 12,000 people worldwide and sales exceeded more than US$1.2 billion last year. Based in the U.S., it operates 14 manufacturing plants in 11 states. It also has 21 plants,

* The author wishes to express sincere appreciation to the advice given by Dr. Cao Yong, Dr. Chen Kang and Associate Professor J. J. Williams.

including three joint ventures, in 12 other countries. Geographically, the company is organised into three units: North America; Europe; and Asia Pacific and Latin America. The office in Singapore is the sales, marketing and warehousing centre for Asia including emerging markets like India, Indochina and China.

Factory Visit and Meeting with Factory Manager and General Manager of Zhongnan Rubber Factory in Chongqing

Zhongnan Rubber Factory in Chongqing which is a state-owned factory, started its operation in 1940. It started with production of low pressure industrial hose, industrial V, conveyor and fan belts as well as some automotive rubber products like the air brake hose. After acquiring three American braiders, it went into manufacturing of medium pressure hydraulic hose. This hose plant is said to have a capacity of 500,000 metres per year, producing up to two-inch inner diameter of 50 metres lengths. Its sales turnover for hose last year was reportedly RMB 100 million. Of this volume, 70% came from Sichuan province, 15% from surrounding provinces like Yunnan and Guichou, and the balance from other provinces.

Presently, they have three shopfloors, one each for belts, automotive and hydraulic hoses manufacturing. Because of cash flow problems, production has stopped. Construction of a new four-level factory space is also half completed. It has a floor area of about 10,000 square metres.

Economic Outlook in China

China's economic record over the past 15 years is legendary: an average 9% annual growth rate since 1978 and a doubling of per capita income in the ten-year period between 1977 and 1987 – an accomplishment which took the U.S. about 50 years to achieve. In 1992, its GNP grew by 12.9% to US$420 billion while 1993 saw a growth of 13.0% to US$633.2 billion.

Purpose and Scope

The most important issue for investors is to determine the best means of investment in order to minimise risks. As a preliminary study, this project aims to examine the best entry strategy into the China market for Gates rubber hose products which are used in almost all industries, especially the construction, oil and gas, transportation, steel and mining industries.

ENTRY STRATEGIES

Export-Oriented Approach

(i) ***Export to Appointed Distributors***: This represents the simplest form of market penetration. The Singapore office would simply export to the appointed distributors. Thus, the most important task is the selection of distributors. If good ones are appointed, then one can expect consistently growing business from them without much intervention. On the other hand, if the opposite happens, then the reputation goes down the drain from day one.

Field trips have to be made by the regional salesperson to identify suitable candidates for distributorship appointments. Apart from their expertise in the field of selling hose, other factors like their location, their annual sales volume, the nature and strength of the industrial base and, of course, their relationships and contacts with customers have to be taken into consideration. Care must be taken not to have distributors covering the same territories or industries.

(ii) ***Location of Distributors:*** Based on the priority investment areas created by the Chinese government, it naturally would be ideal to have distributors situated there. Gates could set up a distributor network to cover the three zones. The distributors, in turn, then have to establish their dealer networks to reach out to remote areas.

Gates should capitalise on the fact that it already has one distributor each in Hong Kong and Taiwan for more than a decade. It would be interesting for these two well-established distributors to service southern China where the SEZs are. Then it would be necessary to have at least one more stockist to cover the ETDZs and the COEA. Shanghai, which is the hub of communications and transport, should be a good location for this distributor to be based. It is China's largest port and second largest aviation centre. Its freight handling capability represents about one-third of the country's total capacity. It also provides river transportation up the Yangtze River as far as Sichuan province. Shanghai is also linked by railways to most parts of China.

Domestic Market Approach

(i) ***Sales Office(s) in China:*** In this option, Gates would take over the role of the distributor. It would actually establish its own sales subsidiary, thereby exporting to itself in China and controlling the marketing programme there. However, this approach involves more than just looking for the right location. Recruiting the right people for the jobs is equally vital.

As far as location is concerned, the approach to sourcing suitable distributors still applies, i.e., we still need good locations for ease of commercial distribution. Hong Kong and Shanghai should still be considered seriously. The high property prices in these locations could prove to be a stumbling block though. The company might consider putting one Singapore staff member in the north and a HongKonger in Hong Kong itself, to run the two offices. Of course, these two area managers would need to recruit some local sales staff to cover a foreseeable extensive dealer network across the country.

(ii) ***Dealer Network:*** Ideally, all the major industrial and economic zones should be covered by one dealer each. For example, the 5 SEZs and the 27 ETDZs can each have a Gates dealer. This distribution concept can be further developed into a co-operative partnership in that all dealers could be given a Gates crimping machine to do the final assembly of hose and couplings. This way, the imported hose and couplings may be exempted from import duties that could otherwise lead to high landed costs.

Manufacturing

The main objective of setting up a manufacturing base in China is to produce a more competitively priced product in order to tap a bigger market share. By enjoying the tax incentives and the cheap labour, this could be a sound alternative.

There are various forms of manufacturing available. Contract manufacturing and licensing have to be ruled out as China does not have the technology to produce products of the quality that Gates requires.

A joint venture involves looking for the right partner. One such candidate was Zhongnan Rubber Factory in Chongqing that had expressed interests in a tie-up with Gates. Unfortunately, their interests did not stop at acquiring Gates technology. They also expected Gates to relieve them of the financial problems that they were facing. Gates has three other companies to consider. They are located in Guangzhou, Xian and Shenyang. Thus far, the one in Shenyang has considered a possible joint venture. It definitely warrants at least a visit.

Wholly-owned manufacturing in China can take the form of acquisition of an existing producer or starting a plant from the ground up. As in a JV, the choices for acquisition are limited to the same four factories. The fact that they are all state-owned can make the process of taking them over very complicated. In the same vein, starting a new production operation in a new market without a customer base is a risky proposition.

Statistics show that of the more than 160,000 foreign funded enterprises, 77.9% are joint ventures, 12.6% are wholly owned and the balance is co-operative partnerships (State Statistical Bureau). Clearly, this shows a strong preference for joint venture investments in China.

DISCUSSION

Basically, every method described above has its strengths and weaknesses. These are briefly discussed next.

Direct Export Versus Own Sales Office

By exporting direct to distributors, Gates could enter the market with a perceived customer base of appointed agents right from the beginning. Through its own sales subsidiary, it has to start looking for its first customer to sell the first foot of hose.

On the other hand, a sales office would have full control of its marketing programmes like pricing strategy and promotional activities whereas the distributors may do it quite differently. This is of vital concern because Gates' policy of projecting itself as a world class manufacturer of rubber hose and belts may not be successfully transferred into the China market.

In terms of profit margins, selling to dealers or end users cuts down on one level of distribution and it will definitely provide better returns than supplying to distributors.

Joint Venture Versus Wholly Owned Manufacturing

Both approaches share about the same investment incentives but a JV seems to have more advantages. China's bureaucracy is such that approvals, say to build a factory, can often take months and may require more than a hundred stamps of endorsements by various authorities. To avoid going through the formalities and procedures in setting up a plant, a JV is the solution.

Also, the customer base of the potential partner carries heavy weightage in helping the management to decide if such a venture is at all feasible. The importance of their relationships (*guanxi*) with customers cannot be over emphasised.

One potential problem for a JV is the decision-making process by the management which will comprise senior officers from both sides. They represent two different companies and decision-making becomes more complex. Wholly owned companies which have full control of the business will not have this problem.

One fear about a JV is that the local partner may become a competitor. During the period of partnership, Gates may transfer enough expertise and technology such that the local partner can survive independently.

RECOMMENDATIONS

Since manufacturing involves a higher capital outlay, it is likely to take a longer time than the first two options. To capitalise on the booming industries that have created a serious shortage of suppliers, it is recommended that sourcing of suitable distributors be carried out immediately so that direct sales can be clinched. However, high import duties can cause the landed costs to be non-competitive. But selling on Gates' quality, as well as product range (Gates' spiral hose in this case) that are not being produced locally should counteract this setback. It seems likely that only the very high pressure spiral hose range will be competitive.

The second option of selling direct to dealers by setting up our own offices may enable Gates to import the full range. However, it may not be feasible since the difference in cost of production in China versus the U.S. can still be very wide. A more detailed study is called for.

While these proposals may help Gates gain some sales, the actual market share may be negligible. Local manufacturing should still be a long term plan. As far as joint ventures are concerned, the four choices that are available should be evaluated. Gates should actively pursue the possibility of a joint ventureship to take advantage of the benefits which a local partner can provide. Much work has to be done to study the potential partner's business philosophy, financial position, market presence, existing equipment as well as the skills and trainability of the workforce.

CONCLUSION

There are many ways of penetrating the China market for any product. Exporting directly to appointed distributors, setting up local sales office, or manufacturing, all have their pros and cons. It was strongly recommended that Gates start by exporting direct to its distributors or its own sales office while simultaneously looking for a suitable joint venture partner. China is simply too huge to be covered in one trip. More follow-up trips have to be taken to formulate plans to execute the various methods.

REFERENCES

Allen Jamie, *Business Asia*, 4 January 1994.

Hua Dai, "Feeling the Strain — Shanghai", *China Economic Review*, April 1994, pp. 25–6.

Terpstra Vern, *International Marketing*, Fourth Edition, The Dryden Press, Fort Worth, 1993.

Trade and Investment Guide — China, Singapore Trade Development Board and Arthur Andersen, 1994.

Wu Gordon, "The Word of Wu", *China Economic Review*, December 1993, pp. 22–3.

F E E D B A C K   F O R M

Thank you for purchasing the Nanyang Business Report series. In order to aid us with the development of other similar books in the future, please give us your opinion in this form and fax or mail it to us at the address given on the back. We would also like to include your name in our mailing list to keep you informed of book promotions which we may have in the future.

Name: ______________________ Occupation: ______________________

Company: ______________________ Type of business: ______________________

Address: ____

____

Do you normally purchase this kind of book? ❑ Yes ❑ No

Which title did you buy? ______________________

Why? ____

How did you learn about this book? ❑ courses/seminars ❑ recommended text

❑ bookshop ❑ advertisements ❑ Others(please specify) ______________

What business magazines are you subscribing to? ______________________

____

What seminars do you normally attend? ______________________

What suggestions for improvement would you recommend to the book you bought?

____

____

What kind of areas do you think we should focus on in business publishing?

____

Why? ____

____

Would you like to be part of our direct mail/mailing list? ❑ Yes ❑ No

Please list out subject areas ______________________

Would you like to aid us in our publishing decision by being a reviewer of unpublished works? ❑ Yes ❑ No

Please list out subject areas if different from above ______________________

____

Please fax to:

The Managing Editor, Simon & Schuster (Asia) Pte Ltd, fax: 3780 371 or email your response to prenhall@singnet.com.sg

FOLD HERE

FOLD HERE

AFFIX
STAMP

The Managing Editor
Simon & Schuster (Asia) Pte Ltd
317 Alexandra Road
#04-01 IKEA Building
Singapore 159965